ORWELL'S LONDON

ORWELL'S LONDON

JOHN THOMPSON

PHOTOGRAPHS BY PHILIPPA SCOONES

SCHOCKEN BOOKS
NEW YORK

First American edition published by Schocken Books 1985
10 9 8 7 6 5 4 3 2 1 85 86 87 88
Published by agreement with Fourth Estate Limited, London

Library of Congress Cataloging in Publication Data

Thompson, John.
  Orwell's London.
  Includes index.
  1. Orwell, George, 1903 – 1950 — Homes and haunts —
England — London. 2. Orwell, George 1903 – 1950 —
Knowledge — England. 3. London (England) — Biography. 4.
London (England) in literature. I. Title.
PR6029.R8Z83 1985 828'.91209 [B] 84 – 23465

Manufactured in Great Britain
ISBN 0 8052 3965 0

ACKNOWLEDGEMENTS

This book could not have been written before the publication of Professor Bernard Crick's biography of Orwell, which for the first time fixed the co-ordinates of his life. In a more general way Robert Hewison's *Under siege: literary life in London 1939-45* (Weidenfeld & Nicolson, 1977) has been of great value. I am especially grateful too to Michael Barsley, Queenie Jeffrey, Michael Mason and René Quinault, whose inspirations and good-will have been invaluable. I also wish to thank: David Astor, Lord Brockway, Margaret Collins, M. Easton, J. D. Farnfield, Margaret French, Tosco Fyvel, Peter Goolden, Richard Graham, Stephen Green, Roger Harrison, Pat Haynes, Daryl Logan, Peter Malins, Lesley Marshall, Ian S. Moore, Jock Murray, J. A. Patron, S. C. Phipp, Vernon Richards, D. W. Riley, Mr and Mrs George Sceeny, Louis Simmonds, Jim Smith, S. R. Somjee, Sir Stephen Spender, M. D. Trace, and George Woodcock.

Acknowledgement is made to the estate of the late Sonia Brownell Orwell for quotation from: George Orwell, *Collected essays, journalism and letters*, vols. I–IV, eds. Ian Angus and Sonia Orwell, Secker & Warburg, 1969; *Down and out in Paris and London*, Secker & Warburg, 1949; *A clergyman's daughter*, Secker & Warburg, 1960; *Keep the aspidistra flying*, Secker & Warburg, 1954; *The road to Wigan Pier*, Secker & Warburg, 1959; *Nineteen eighty-four*, Secker & Warburg, 1949.

A. J. Ayer, *Part of my life*, Collins, 1977; Mark Benney, *Almost a gentleman*, Peter Davis, 1966; Jacintha Buddicom, *Eric and us*, Frewin, 1974; Anthony Burgess, *1985*, Hutchinson, 1978; Jack Common Collection, University of Newcastle; Jack Common, *Stand*, vol. 22, no. 3; Cyril Connolly, *Encounter*, January 1962; Cyril Connolly, *The evening colonnade*, David Bruce & Watson, 1973; Lettice Cooper, memoir, Orwell Archive; Bernard Crick, *George Orwell: a life*, Secker & Warburg, 1981; Avril Dunn, *Twentieth Century*, March 1961; Elisaveta Fen, *Twentieth Century*, August 1960; Constantine Fitzgibbon, *The life of Dylan Thomas*, Dent, 1975; T. R. Fyvel, *George Orwell: a memoir*, Weidenfeld & Nicolson, 1982; Graham Greene, *Penguin New Writing*, no. 9, 1941; Graham Greene, *Ways of escape*, Bodley Head, 1980; Rayner Heppenstall, *Twentieth Century*, April 1955; Rayner Heppenstall, *Four absentees*, Barrie & Rockcliff, 1960; Tom Hopkinson, *The Cornhill*, Summer 1953; Denis King-Farlow, memoir, Orwell Archive; Michael MacDonagh, *In London during the Great War*, Eyre & Spottiswoode, 1935; Julian Maclaren-Ross, *Memoirs of the forties*, Alan Ross, 1965; John Morris, *Penguin New Writing*, no. 40, 1950; Malcolm Muggeridge, *Chronicles of wasted time*, vol. II, Collins, 1973; Malcolm Muggeridge, *Like it was*, Collins, 1981; *Orwell remembered*, eds. Audrey Coppard and Bernard Crick, Ariel, 1984; Ruth Pitter, memoir, Orwell Archive; Paul Potts, *Dante called you Beatrice*, Eyre & Spottiswoode, 1960; Anthony Powell, *To keep the ball rolling*, Heinemann, 1976; Richard Rees, *Fugitive from the camp of victory*, Secker & Warburg, 1961; Julian Symons, *Critical occasions*, Hamish Hamilton, 1966; Fredric Warburg, *An occupation for gentlemen*, Hutchinson, 1959; Fredric Warburg, *All authors are equal*, Hutchinson, 1973; George Woodcock, *Northern Review*, August–September 1953; George Woodcock, *The crystal spirit*, Fourth Estate, 1984; *The world of George Orwell*, ed. Miriam Gross, Weidenfeld & Nicolson, 1971.

Archive illustrations are from the following sources: BBC Hulton Picture Library, pp 25, 29, 30, 34, 57, 59, 61, 66, 67, 78, 93, 95, 110–12; Estate of Rayner Heppenstall, p.94; GLC, pp 23, 24, 26, 27, 31–33, 67, 81, 83; Imperial War Museum, pp 9, 10, 57, 58, 93; Keystone Press, pp 56, 84; Mander & Mitchenson, pp 11, 39; Marylebone Cricket Club, p.10; Orwell Archive, pp 53, 103; Salvation Army p. 28; Sir Osbert Lancaster p.109; Teachers' World, p.69; Topham Picture Library, p.26; University of London, p.69; Vernon Richards, cover & p.92; Westminster Library, pp 79, 113.

CONTENTS

TO THE WOMEN OF BRITAIN.

1. You have read what the Germans have done in Belgium. Have you thought what they would do if they invaded this Country **?**

2. Do you realise that the safety of your home and children depends on our getting more men **NOW** **?**

3. Do you realise that the one word "GO" from you may send another man to fight for our King and Country **?**

4. When the War is over and someone asks your husband or your son what he did in the great War, is he to hang his head because you would not let him go **?**

WON'T YOU HELP AND SEND A MAN TO JOIN THE ARMY TO-DAY?

1

A LITTLE LESS THAN A MAN

When the First World War began, Eric Blair, who was later to call himself George Orwell, was eleven years old, while his father was settled down in retirement. Neither was of the age to be a soldier. Eric was old enough, though, to be carried along on England's wave of patriotism:

> Awake! Oh you young men of England
> For if when your country's in need
> You do not enlist by the thousand
> You truly are cowards indeed.

These are his first published lines. He was still young enough when the war ended to have escaped conscription, but only at the price of sharing his generation's guilty relief. Near-contemporaries at school had fought and died, and – more immediately – his father had taken up his son's poetic challenge. At sixty he had successfully volunteered for the army.

Mr Blair took ship for Marseilles in 1917, and this decided Eric's mother, Ida, and elder sister, Marjorie, to let the family house at Henley and move to London for wartime employment. They took a flat in a house, now demolished, belonging to a Mrs Brown at 23 Cromwell Crescent in Earl's Court. It lay on the southern side of the Cromwell Road, on the edge of gentility. Mrs Blair found a clerical job at the Ministry of Pensions, then housed on Millbank in the Tate Gallery, and only a short tube ride away, while Marjorie went on to become a dispatch rider. Avril, the baby of the family, was sent to a boarding school in Ealing.

The Great War had transformed the mood of London. Within a week of its outbreak a bill had been hurried through Parliament in anticipation of spies and saboteurs. The city became panicky and paranoid: German bakers were said to be putting slow poison in their bread, German barbers to be cutting their customers' throats. Delicatessen owners felt obliged to label their sausages 'Good English Viands'. Many Germans were interned: nearly a thousand waiters, cooks and tailors were locked in the Alexandra Palace; other aliens, resident and refugee, were shut in the Kensington Olympia and the Earl's Court Exhibition halls for the duration. Orwell later recalled the fierce rejection of all things German – the shunning of German music and even German dogs, the execration of the Kaiser, vulgarly depicted in aggressively patriotic pictures at the Royal Academy.

The so-called Die-Hards – those calling for a complete commitment to victory – set out from the beginning to shame the capital into total war. Association football crowds were met by sandwichboard-men asking them, 'Are You Forgetting There's a War On?' German families, from the king's (Saxe-Coburg-Gotha) downward, were forced by public opinion to change their names. In the East End, the house of a Scotsman called Strachan was sacked because he had a supposedly German-sounding name. Fear of spies and saboteurs was epidemic. The working classes of Battersea believed the marauding Zeppelins were being inflated and launched from their neighbours' back yards. A newspaper reporter at a Die-Hard meeting was denounced as a spy when a woman noticed him using an unfamiliar form of shorthand. As late as August 1918, with the war almost won, a huge procession followed a beflagged lorry from Hyde Park through Oxford Street, Regent Street and Cockspur Street to Trafalgar Square. On the lorry, rolled up like a big drum, were a million and a quarter signatures, petitioning Lloyd George to intern all those aliens still at large. Only a month previously the Prime Minister had announced that he was receiving anonymous letters from Germans in England crowing over British setbacks at the Front. It was assumed by some that they were written by Die-Hards, to inflame moderate opinion.

It was a state of affairs as close to the atmosphere of *Nineteen eighty-four* as England has ever come, certainly more charged with hate and hysteria than the war of 1939–45. Though technologically quite remote (there was no hint of speakwrites and saccharine) it was akin to it in other, unmistakable ways. Lord Kitchener was the nation's father and protector and, stern and infallible, inscrutable behind his moustache, the accusation of his pointing finger could no more be eluded than Big Brother's gaze. Democratic government had quickly atrophied to a tiny War Cabinet, supported by a monstrous bureaucracy. The great government departments churned out new regulations, restrictions, half-truths, exhortations. They offered the English people a choice of self-sacrifice or dishonour and defeat. Families were cajoled to give up their meat, their Bank Holiday, their gardener, their son. The general response was enormous. Women turned hawkish eyes on 'shirkers' hiding in 'funkholes', and spared no-one. An officer awarded the V.C. one morning was presented with the white feather (a derisive badge of cowardice) in the afternoon, when relaxing out of uniform in Hyde Park. There was a nationwide conviction of the Almighty's support for the British cause (so much so that the Dean of St Paul's had to tell his congregation that God must be fed up with their 'pesterings' for victory). Looking back from the Second World War, Orwell remembered the Englishman's readiness at the time to de-humanise his enemy: 'one of the mitigating features of this war is that there has been very little hatred. There has been none of the non-sensical racialism that there was last time – no pretence that all Germans have faces like pigs, for instance.'

A dramatic fall in the crime rate demonstrated the strength of the new sense of national cohesion. Even with the street lamps dim and regular policemen enlisted, the criminal turned patriot. Similarly the idle became industrious. Before the war the Salvation Army was giving food and shelter to 2,000 men and women each night in London. By 1915 there were only a hundred or so. The reason, however, was that many casually-employed youths had joined up, so there was a demand for the labour even of the old and broken, who consequently were able to afford common lodging-houses.

A change of face mirrored London's change of heart. More and more men wore khaki, and the women put on mourning. Air raids began, blacking out the city at night. First the Zeppelins came over, then aero-planes. Londoners were awed by the dreadful wizardry of the airships, falling silent in their cellars for fear of being overheard by the shivering German airmen, thousands of feet up in the night sky. Big Ben was silenced, and the lake in St James's Park drained – this because reflec-ted moonlight on its surface would guide the raiders to Buckingham Palace, the Houses of Parliament and Whitehall. The air-raid pre-cautions were in the charge of the Admiralty and were monolithically organised. Between ten thousand and twenty thousand telephone calls mobilised and demobilised the defences, and boy scouts with bugles shot out on their cycles to sound the all-clear. On the night of one raid, none of the anti-aircraft guns was fired. Parliament was outraged, but assured that silence had been deliberately kept, so as not to betray the position of London to the enemy.

'As I go about', a *Times* journalist noted privately in 1916, 'I can see the wide spaciousness of London and its vast variety of characteristics slowly but surely contracting to a War Camp.' Two-storey war buildings went up on St James's Park accommodating the Admiralty; new hutments on Regent's Park were used for the Military Postal Depot, sending and receiving millions of letters to and from the Front. Hotels, such as the Cecil and the Metropole, were commandeered for the armed services. The voice of the drill sergeant was to be heard from morning until night in the royal parks, the gardens of the inns of court, and in the squares. Guards of soldiers stood at all the railway stations.

The cost of the war rose steadily, from five, to six, to seven million pounds a day, and London's leisure was gradually cut back. It was decided to close down many of the museums and art galleries to save a little money and release the staff for the army. The Eton and Harrow match, the University Boat Race, and the Chelsea Flower Show were all suspended, though at the 1915 annual Daffodil Show in the Horticultural Hall, Westminster, there was a new variety, the 'Lord Kitchener', described by its exhibitor as 'a bold, well-balanced flower, a tall grower'. The emergency Defence of the Realm Act, known as Dora, affected everyone: licensing hours were cut (and have remained so); eating-houses were forced to restrict the size of their meals to two courses for lunch and three for dinner (though on Christmas Day the quota could be reversed); the showing of lights at night was forbidden, while a curfew order was introduced on places of entertainment, to save coal. There were unexpected scarcities: only enough matches for one box per adult per week. Meat rationing was introduced, and with great success, evening out distribution to the advantage of the labouring classes. To counter the food shortage, London's waste land was turned over to garden allotments; potatoes, cabbages, parsnips and carrots were planted around the Queen Victoria Memorial at Buckingham Palace.

Eric, meanwhile, with his father at war and his mother and sister swelling the ranks of women workers, lived in what he always thought to be the 'tolerant and civilised atmosphere' of Eton. The headmaster there caused a storm of anger and protest early in the war when he preached a sermon at St Margaret's church in Westminster, asking that the enemy be fought without hatred. 'If we are going to act as a Christian nation we are bound to apply true Christian charity on a scale to which we have never risen before. . . . There is no other question in the War comparable to this for greatness.' So deep was the public resentment at these words, that he had to make a further statement, amounting to a retraction: 'I believe the German spirit, as now manifested, to be an utterly dangerous and abominable thing, and that the hope for peace and honour among mankind rests, so far as I can see, in a decisive victory of the Allies'.

Eric's visits to the spiritual and material austerities of London would seem to have been restricted, because his mother felt unable to accommodate her children for any length of time in her cramped quarters in Earl's Court. In November 1917 she contacted a family friend in Oxfordshire called Mrs Buddicom: 'I am writing to ask a *great* favour of you, which I hope you will not hesitate to refuse if you cannot see your way to doing it for me. I want to know if you will be so very kind as to have Eric and Avril for their Xmas holidays as paying guests. I am very awkwardly placed . . .' As it was a satisfactory arrangement on both sides, the request was repeated the following year: 'do you think you could have Eric and Avril for the Xmas holidays, they have implored me to ask you. . . ?' This was sent from a new, but similarly small, flat off Notting Hill Gate, 23 Mall Chambers. So again Eric and his sister went not to London but to Oxfordshire for Christmas, pursued by presents from their mother:

My dear Mrs. Buddicom
 I sent off a parcel directed to you yesterday with some Xmas presents which please give to the children on Xmas morning. Avril always has a stocking so I put in a few odds & ends for it . . . & will you please give Eric 25/- from his father & 6/- from his Aunt Nellie & Avril 4/- from her Aunt Nellie.

This was December 1918 and the war was just over, Eric's participation having been limited to eating margarine instead of butter. While his family fought and worked for the war and his schoolfellows fought and died, he had not taken the test. Later he wrote, 'my particular generation, those who had been "just too young", became conscious of the vastness of the experience they had missed. You felt yourself a little less than a man, because you had missed it.' In future years Orwell was often to suggest that his life was driven by a complex motor of guilt, and his part in the Great War may have been a component of it. It probably influenced his decision to prolong his boyhood no further, after Eton, by going to Oxford, but to sail instead to Burma and a policeman's responsibilities. Almost certainly it lay behind his move to

London at the beginning of the next war, and his determination to participate as fully as possible in the battle on the Home Front.

Mrs Blair kept on the flat at Notting Hill as a *pied-à-terre* until 1921, and now, with the pressures of war removed, Eric seems to have been able to make fuller use of it. He stayed there each July when he came up to Town for the Eton versus Harrow cricket match, that fixture now having been resumed. Mrs Buddicom's son Prosper was at Harrow, so her family went up too and stayed at the Langham Hotel, meeting Eric, suitably and showily dressed for the occasion, at Lord's. Jacintha, Prosper's brother and just a little older than Eric, remembers that

'Lord's' in those days was always a terrific social occasion, with all the mothers and sisters dressed in their best, [while] people who had them used their coaches – not modern motor-coaches, but fine four-in-hands or brakes, which were open-topped, with a lot of seats for a big party and extravagant picnic hampers. I don't think even in those days, many people actually *drove up* in the coaches, these were to Cut a Dash, traditionally impressive: they would have driven up in the Rollses and Daimlers and Bentleys.

In 1920 (when Eton won after making a big first innings lead) Jacintha's Uncle John stood everyone salmon and champagne, but was chagrined because Jacintha paid him no attention, 'enjoying flirtations' instead with Eric. These flirtations were either *wild* or *mild* – Jacintha's aunt's handwriting is uncertain. It was at that match too that Eric showed unrepeated entrepreneurial flair, publishing and selling an issue of an Eton magazine, *College Days*, with a friend and netting £128, more than he was to earn for many pages of journalism in impecunious left-wing papers. The collaborator, Denys King-Farlow, says the issue was 'heavy with snob-appeal advertisements': 'The Hot Spot Chalmers America's Favourite Six'; '*De Reszke* – the Aristocrat of Cigarettes'; 'The Sizaire-Berwick Automobile'; 'Palmers Cord Tyres – the highest price tyres – and deservedly so'. Orwell returned to Lord's in June 1940, twenty years after leaving Eton, as a member of the newly-formed Local Defence Volunteers. In his diary he wrote: 'Last time I was at Lord's must have been at the Eton-Harrow match in 1921. At that time I should have felt that to go into the Pavilion, not being a member of the MCC, was on a par with pissing on the altar, and years later would have had some vague idea that it was a legal offence for which you could be prosecuted.'

In 1920 Marjorie brought a friend to the flat at Mall Chambers, the young poet Ruth Pitter, five years older than Eric, who was nearing the end of his time at Eton. She remembered her visit well:

The outer doors of the flats opened almost directly into the sitting-rooms. So the moment our hostess let us in I saw a tall youth, with hair the colour of hay and a brown tweed suit, standing at a table by the window, cleaning a sporting gun. There was something arresting in the way he looked up. His eyes were blue and rather formidable, and an exact pair.

He was thinking, he told her much later, 'I wonder if that girl would be hard to get.'

Two years later, perhaps from a sense of duty, perhaps a young man's sense of adventure, Blair sailed for Burma and a job in the Imperial Police – 'five boring years within the sound of bugles', he later complained. When he returned, one of the first people he was to write to, to her surprise, was Ruth Pitter.

Mrs Brown's house, 23 Cromwell Crescent, was demolished in the 1960s when the Cromwell Road was widened. But these original houses on the northern side are intact.

Mall Chambers, Notting Hill Gate, W11. Mrs Blair's second London flat was on the third floor of this block. Notting Hill Gate is on the Circle Line, so Millbank and the Tate Gallery would have been easily accessible to her.

Temporary war buildings on the Victoria Embankment gardens, SW1. Hutments such as these filled London's open spaces during World War I. Orwell was well aware of the physical changes in London life during this war, and Nineteen eighty-four *should not automatically be associated simply with the 1940s.*

A 'Victory Loan' rally in Trafalgar Square, World War I. No picture could better illustrate the perspective the war gave to Orwell's final fictional description of life in Britain.

'Blood and Iron', by Charles Ernest Butler, RA. This Royal Academy painting, one of the many illustrating the devilish nature of the Kaiser, was a symptom of a chauvinistic fervour which Orwell observed to be absent during the next war.

The Eton versus Harrow match early this century. Then, as in Orwell's time, it was a decorous and highly fashionable occasion.

The blue lagoon *at the Prince of Wales theatre, Coventry Street, W1. Eric and Prosper went to a matinee performance of H. de Vere Stacpoole's play on 28th December 1920, and* The beggar's opera *at the Lyric, Hammersmith, the following day.* The blue lagoon *had opened at the Prince of Wales Theatre in August that year, and it was hailed by the critics as a tour de force of staging.* The Daily Graphic *said that 'Playgoers have rarely seen greater ingenuity or more artistic effects in scenic illustration. The Fire at Sea, the Drifting of the Boat, the Island of the Blue Lagoon, the Storm – all these were deservedly applauded.' The story-line was as daring as the scenery, culminating in the imminent consummation of young – under age – love. The* Times *nobly tried to dissuade the prurient: 'could not possibly give offence'.*

2

DOWN AND OUT

In July 1927, five years after arriving there, Blair made a break from Burma. He took five months' leave in England and made up his mind not to return; his resignation was registered from the beginning of 1928. He lived at first with his family in Southwold, his father aging, his sister Avril now working in a local teashop, but he had made up his mind to move to London, to live on the money he had saved in the East and begin a career as a writer. So, some time late in 1927 he wrote to Ruth Pitter, who was then working in a pottery studio in Notting Hill and living with a woman friend in Portobello Road: 'To my surprise I had a letter from him at this time, asking if I remembered him. He wanted us to find him a cheap lodging.' She found him one, next door to the studio's Portobello Road workshop. The aspiring writer moved in:

I have a clear picture in my mind of Orwell lugging some heavy suitcases into our workshop house; no doubt to sort out the contents more easily than he could have done in the cramped bedroom next door. He was now a very tall man; he had the same rather formidable, perhaps defensive, look; and the very wide *terai* hat he was still wearing made him look still more imposing.

He looked to her far from well even then, and she thought he must have suffered, after years in the Burmese heat, from his first English winter – a particularly cold one. His room was unheated, 'though we did, rather belatedly, lend him an oil-stove. He said afterwards that he used to light a candle to try and warm his hands when they were too numb to write.' His unfeeling landlady was a Mrs Edwin Craig. While her lodger froze within, she liked to keep up appearances. In 1944 Orwell told a little story about her for the benefit of the readers of *Tribune*.

Years ago I lodged for a while in the Portobello Road. This is hardly a fashionable quarter, but the landlady had been lady's maid to some woman of title and had a good opinion of herself. One day something went wrong with the front door and my landlady, her husband and myself were all locked out of the house. It was evident that we should have to get in by an upper window, and as there was a jobbing builder next door I suggested borrowing a ladder from him. My landlady looked somewhat uncomfortable.

'I wouldn't like to do that,' she said finally. 'You see we don't know him. We've been here fourteen years, and we've always taken care not to know the people on either side of us. It *wouldn't do*, not in a neighbourhood like this. If you once begin talking to them they get familiar, you see.'

So we had to borrow a ladder from a relative of her husband's and carry it nearly a mile with great discomfort.

That winter, cold and short of money, Blair was already trying to project his experience into fiction. The miserable couple in an early play receive bills one morning amounting almost to £40. They have 7s 4d in hand, and if their baby doesn't have an expensive operation it will die. Years later, as a literary editor, Orwell was to complain of being over-exposed to the kind of story that begins, 'Marjorie's husband was to be hanged on Tuesday, and the children were starving', or 'For seven years no ray of sunlight had penetrated the dusty room where William Grocock, a retired insurance agent, lay dying of cancer', but this sort of thing was at present his own forte.

He was sharpening his resolve to cut himself more completely adrift, to become not merely a persecuted bourgeois, but a spectacularly disreputable outcast. It was a way of escape from the pressures of life on the margin of the middle class, and excellent copy too.

I thought it over and decided what I would do. I would go suitably disguised to Limehouse and Whitechapel and such places and sleep in common lodging-houses and pal up with dock labourers, street hawkers, derelict people, beggars, and, if possible, criminals. And I would find out about tramps and how you got in touch with them and what was the proper procedure for entering the casual ward; and then, when I felt that I knew the ropes well enough, I would go on the road myself.

Limehouse, near the West India Docks, was his first choice. Now it is redeveloped with housing estates, but then it had an exotic reputation as London's Chinatown. In the late nineteenth century the Chinese were a picturesque feature of the locality, with their pigtails and loads on long poles over their shoulders, but by Orwell's time Limehouse Causeway and Pennyfields, where they chiefly lived, were drab and sombre thoroughfares. In fact, there never had been more than about three hundred resident Chinese there, and all males, who often took English wives. But to the visitor there was a *frisson* nevertheless, partly due to Thomas Burke's popular mystifications of the area in his fictions: 'The shuttered gloom of the quarter showed strangely menacing. Every whispering house seemed an abode of dread things, every window seemed filled with frightful eyes. Every corner half lit by the bleak light of a naked gas-jet seemed to harbour unholy things, and a sense of danger hung on every step.' So daring students would go to try their skill with chopsticks and eat a death-defying meal in one of Limehouse Causeway's retaurants. White slavery, racketeering and violence Chinese-style were a thrilling sauce to the authentic oriental cuisine. 'Despite the vigilance of the police,' said one guidebook, 'opium dens and fan-tan saloons still exist, but it is not wise for the visitor to see these establishments from the inside.' In truth, life was much more banal and domestic than outsiders would have wished to believe, though the local vicar did complain in 1930 that the neighbourhood was occasionally demoralised by epidemics of fantan and puckapu. Any violence that was coming to an Old Etonian with an undisguisable accent and doubtfully plausible hard-luck story would be from the stevedores and deck-hands that the docks brought to the area.

Before making his expedition he had first to dress himself correctly, and so bought an outfit from one of Lambeth's many rag shops, dirtied it in what he thought were appropriate places, and changed into it – not in his landlady's respectable house, but next door at Ruth Pitter's. Then he walked all the way east to stop in front of a dark, dirty-looking lodging-house in Limehouse Causeway. Fully expecting instant recognition as an intruder and an ensuing fight, and as though, he said, going into a sewer full of rats, he stepped inside, down to a frowsy firelit kitchen underground:

There were stevedores and navvies and a few sailors sitting about and playing draughts and drinking tea. They barely glanced at me as I entered. But this was Saturday night and a hefty young stevedore was drunk and was reeling about the room. He turned, saw me, and lurched towards me with broad red face thrust out and a dangerous-looking fishy gleam in his eyes. I stiffened myself. So the fight was coming already! The next moment the stevedore collapsed on my chest and flung his arms round my neck. ''Ave a cup of tea, chum!' he cried tearfully; ''ave a cup of tea!'

It was 'a kind of baptism' he wrote; but crucifixion was to follow.* The bed he found not only hard, small, cold and horribly smelly, but also

---

*Orwell's accounts of dossing in Limehouse are fragmentary and somewhat contradictory, but are pieced together here.

convex, so that he had to hold on all night to avoid falling out. A man in the corner suffered from unspeakably repellent coughing fits. Once he struck a match and Orwell saw he was a very old man, 'wearing his trousers wrapped round his head as a nightcap, a thing which for some reason disgusted me very much'. There was a sailor in the bed next to Orwell's who every so often woke up, swore vilely, and lit a cigarette. At each cough or oath a voice from another bed cried out: 'Shut up! Oh, for Christ's —— *sake* shut up!' Going to wash, after an inevitably broken night, a lucky piece of soap in his pocket, he found that 'every basin was streaked with grime – solid, sticky filth as black as boot-blacking'. He went out unwashed into the Limehouse streets, 'Sprinkled with Orientals – Chinamen, Chittagonian lascars, Dravidians selling silk scarves, even a few Sikhs, come goodness knows how.'

The East End Sunday mornings were alive with activity, Christian religious and Jewish secular. On the East India Dock Road the Salvation Army sang 'Anybody here like sneaking Judas?' to the tune of 'What's to be done with the drunken sailor?'; in Whitechapel The Singing Evangel offered salvation for sixpence, and there was an unruly Mormon gathering on Tower Hill. In Petticoat Lane the working classes were in holiday mood:

In Middlesex Street, among the crowds at the market, a draggled, down-at-heel woman was hauling a brat of five by the arm. She brandished a tin trumpet in its face. The brat was squalling.

'Enjoy yourself!' yelled the mother. 'What yer think I brought yer out 'ere for an' brought y'a trumpet an' all? D'ya want to go across my knee? You little bastard, you *shall* enjoy yerself!'

Some drops of spittle fell from the trumpet. The mother and child disappeared, both bawling.

It was always Orwell's intention, once he felt he knew the ropes, to explore the casual wards. These were local authority institutions, often a wing of the workhouse, accomodating and feeding 'destitute wayfarers and wanderers'. To live in them was to touch bottom: however nauseating London's lowest class of lodging houses might be, they retained at least vestiges of dignity. The lodgers paid for their beds, they could smoke, cook, play games, drink, sing and enjoy the atmosphere of the communal kitchens. At the casual wards, or 'spikes', there was no such frowsy brotherliness. The London County Council congratulated itself on the combination of utility, discipline and luxury it offered:

At a casual ward a man may obtain a clean lodging; he is given a hot bath, a proper bed in a heated cubicle or dormitory, and clean night clothing, and subsequently he is given facilities for washing and repairing his clothes. For his lodging in a casual ward, a casual is by law required to do a certain amount of work and to remain in the ward for a period of 1 to 4 days according to whether he has been admitted to a ward in the local authority area more than once in a period of a month.

The manual work, however, could be dispensed with 'in certain circumstances', and in practice the tramps were usually discharged on the morning following their admission, unless they were found to be living too freely on the bounty of the ratepayers, in which case they were kept locked in – so the authorities did not really think that the casual ward was the tramp's ideal of where he should be: to be kept there longer than overnight was a punishment.

In fact, the price for a free bed was high. Tobacco had to be smuggled in; a man with drink on his breath could be imprisoned; anyone found with more than eightpence in hand was in trouble. The hot bath, Orwell discovered, was merely an opportunity to sit in solutions of other people's dirt. The atmosphere was smelly, and needlessly regimented: on one occasion the supper bread had been cut the night before and was so hard the hungry tramps could only mumble at it.

It isn't easy to understand why Orwell should have courted such degradation. He wrote afterwards that it was by way of atonement for imperial sins, but it seems too that community through hardship was an attraction. More than anything he felt a sense of release: from the upward, individualistic pressures of his education, from the moral strain of his duties and indulgences in Burma, from the perception of a precarious foothold in his class, and, most certainly, from the uncertainties of his chosen career as a writer. By going 'where there is no getting of jobs or losing of jobs, no relatives or friends to plague you, no hope, fear, ambition, honour, duty' he was making a preemptive strike on failure.

In the spring of 1928 he gave up his room in the Portobello Road and went to Paris, tempted perhaps by years of cultural starvation, the promise of a creative ambience, and by a brief taste of the life there when stopping over on the way back from Burma. It was, after his life on the bourgeois margin and the edge of society itself, another exercise in declassing himself. He went almost at the end of the time when unknown writers were ten a penny. Within a year or two the slump was to descend, leaving the huge Montparnasse cafes deserted. He left after eighteen months and returned to England in late 1929, now truly poor, his savings spent, to live again with his parents in Southwold.

The tramping was resumed, but hampered now by the financial necessity of living away from London. He built up instead a little rota of London friends whose houses he could use to stay in and to change identity. By 1930 Ruth Pitter and her colleague had moved to Chelsea and a business of their own:

Orwell used to turn up now and then. He liked our large workshop. I remember his changing into very shabby clothes in its shadowy recesses, prior to some excursion into the seamy side of life. He didn't look in the least like a poor man. God knows he *was* poor, but the formidable look didn't go with the rags. He left in the workshop a suitcase full of clothes – to our feminine eyes the most deplorable clothes. He would write from time to time and ask for various choice items to be sent on.

It was time of anger and anguish for Orwell, when he lived the life of his own Gordon Comstock, socially hypersensitive, and financially perverse with women. He sometimes asked Ruth Pitter to go out with him:

I have lively recollections of these occasions, at the same time heartrending and comic. You see, he hardly ever had enough money, and it was terrible to him to let a woman pay. I used to take picnic lunches and help as tactfully as I could, but the heartrending element *would* come in. . . . In the bus, I sneak the money for our fares into his hand. Ah, to-day he *has* some money – we have lunch in a restaurant, and even a bottle of wine. Now he is penniless again, and I treat him to a dinner; he is furious, until I remind him that he is the younger person and must put up with it.

Like Comstock too, he was hungrily in search of a living from letters, and the *Adelphi*, an intellectual and literary quarterly, began to carry his reviews. Its editors were Richard Rees and Max Plowman, and to Rees, another Old Etonian, Orwell seemed a pleasant man, though lacking a little in vitality. But to Jack Common, a self-styled proletarian writer, who noted his 'scrub of hair and curiously ravaged face', he was a disappointment. 'He looked the real thing: outcast, gifted pauper, kicker against authority, perhaps near-criminal. But he rose to acknowledge the introduction with a hand-shake. Right away manners – and. . ."breeding" – showed through. A sheep in wolf's clothing I thought'.

In fact, Common was judged just as harshly by Orwell, as he found when they ran into each other at the Plowmans' house in Oakwood Road in Hampstead Garden Suburb. 'Dorothy Plowman was getting us going on a series of games of Badminton. Eric irritated me by constantly apologising for being incorrectly dressed, braces keeping his trousers up instead of a belt. Then after a few games he had to look askance at me: I'd developed blisters from the racket handle which dear Dorothy insisted on dressing – a let down for the working classes obviously.'

Hampstead Garden Surburb, begun in 1906, was intended by Henrietta Barnett to house a socially mixed but harmonious society in quasi-rural surroundings. It was a trendy place to live in the 1920s and '30s, attractive to the middle-class socialist cranks Orwell finds so offensive in *The road to Wigan Pier*, though from whose number he nevertheless accepted help and friendship. At 1b Oakwood Road, up from the Plowmans', lived Mr Francis Fierz and his wife Mabel. Orwell met them in Southwold in 1930, and Mabel took him to her bosom, encouraging and promoting him and giving him the use of their house both as a place from which to launch his tramping expeditions and as somewhere to stay and write. Here, in August 1931, he typed out the first draft of *Down and out in Paris and London* (for which book he first used his pseudonym) and sent it off to a publisher. That done, on 25th August, he went down to either Ruth Pitter's or Richard Rees's, at 33 Cheyne Walk, to change – then stepped into the abyss again. This time he intended to go hop-picking, and was not to reemerge until October.

This most extended of his explorations began at Lewis Levy's kip at 90 – 92 Westminster Bridge Road, involved a further night and a shave in Trafalgar Square, and then one night more in a kip in Southwark Bridge Road before he finally set out for Kent by way of a twopenny tram to Bromley. After three weeks of happiness and hard work in the hopfields he returned to London by the cheap hoppers' train to London Bridge station that took nearly five hours to cover the thirty miles to London. Immediately he made for Bermondsey, where Lew Levy had another lodging house: 'probably the best sevenpenny one in London. There are bugs in the beds, but not many'.

Bermondsey was a working-class borough fed by the Thameside wharves and warehouses around Tower Bridge. It specialised in smelly 'offensive trades': tripe-boiling, fellmongering, glue-making and fat-melting; corruptive processes of the kind Orwell found peculiarly irresistible. It was a borough even then in decline. The population was falling, the housing deteriorating, while the incidence of tuberculosis was a cause for worry. The local council was nonetheless active and socially-minded, and in 1927 new public baths and washhouses were opened in the Grange Road. It was here Orwell came to soak out the grime of three weeks on the road and in the fields. Now demolished, the building, as the *Official Guide* made clear, was of advanced conception: 'Internally it is the last word in fitting and equipment. . . . The baths are a complete modern establishment in every detail and comprise slipper baths for men and women, two swimming-baths, Turkish and Russian baths, and a public laundry.'

Orwell used his lodging house as a base from which to work in Billingsgate fish market, just over Tower Bridge, going there around 5 am when the market opened and standing about to compete for jobs as a 'scat': helping porters push barrows of fish 'up the 'ill' into Eastcheap: 'The payment is "twopence an up". They take on about one shover-up for four hundredweight, and the work knocks it out of your thighs and elbows, but you don't get enough jobs to tire you out. Standing there from five till nearly midday, I never made more than 1/6d.'

In the afternoons he was trying to write up his recent experiences, and went to the reading room of the Bermondsey public library to do so. But the strain of prolonged exposure to hard manual work, and the dirt, noise and heat of his lodging house were becoming too much, and in the first week of October he wrote home for money. When it came he took a room at 2 Windsor Street, Paddington, owned at the time by one Frederick Patston, in the area next to St Mary's hospital and now replaced by a modern housing estate. He did not stay long but, after a couple of months, moved to Westminster Chambers in Westminster Bridge Road, SE1.

At around the time of this move, Christmas 1931, Orwell made his most audacious social descent: it was his hope to spend a Christmas in gaol. This had been in his mind for some time; he had told Jack Common about it in 1930, when his plan was to have himself imprisoned through lighting a bonfire in Trafalgar Square. Common thought that sounded like an act of immaturity, but Orwell's problem was to find a crime that merited gaol, through nothing serious enough to lead to investigations into his identity. He explained the scheme he had decided on to Richard Rees when, the Saturday before Christmas, he went to his flat and asked him if he might change his clothes. 'Having left his respectable suit in the bedroom, he went off again dressed more or less in rags. He wanted, he said, to know about prison from the inside and he hoped that if he were picked up drunk and disorderly in the East End he might manage to achieve this'. In fact he had partial success only.

That afternoon he took four or five shillings to the Mile End Road, bought a 'Yank mag' and some tobacco against the boredom to come and, as soon as the pubs opened, began systematically to intoxicate himself with beer and then whisky, on an empty stomach. He staggered out along the pavement, his brain clear, he wrote, but his legs and speech gone, hoping to encounter a policeman. For a while he met only with derisive, pointing shoppers, then, finally

I saw two policemen coming. I pulled the whisky bottle out of my pocket and, in their sight, drank what was left, which nearly knocked me out, so that I clutched a lamppost and fell down. The two policemen ran towards me, turned me over and took the bottle out of my hand.

They: ''Ere, what you bin drinking?' (For a moment they may have thought it was a case of suicide.)

I: 'Thass my boll whisky. You lea' me alone.'

They: 'Coo, 'e's fair bin bathing in it! – What you bin doing of, eh?'

I 'Bin in boozer, 'avin' bit o' fun. Christmas, ain't it?'

Like Gordon in *Keep the aspidistra flying*, Orwell was marched off to a police station; Bethnal Green, he later discovered. There he was questioned, had his money, matches, razor and scarf taken away and was locked in a cell on his own until Monday. Through the Sunday he was fed on the official bread, marge and tea, but on unofficial meat and potatoes too, cooked by the sergeant's wife. Early on Monday morning he was given back his scarf and turned out into the station yard where the Black Maria was waiting.

Inside, the Black Maria was just like a French public lavatory, with a row of tiny locked compartments on either side, each just large enough to sit down in. . . . We drove around to various police stations picking up about ten prisoners in all, until the Black Maria was quite full. They were quite a jolly crowd inside. The compartment doors were open at the top, for ventilation, so that you could reach across, and somebody had managed to smuggle matches in, and we all had a smoke. Presently we began singing, and, as it was near Christmas, sang several carols. We drove up to Old Street Police Court singing:

Adeste, fideles, laeti triumphantes,
Adeste, adeste ad Bethlehem etc.

Which seemed to me rather inappropriate.

When Dorothy, in *A clergyman's daughter*, standing outside the same courthouse sees a Black Maria approaching and hears the sound of 'Adeste, fideles' from within, she little guesses her author is inside.

Once in the courthouse Orwell was locked for several hours in a lively communal cell, tried at lighting speed under his false name – 'Edward-Burton-drunk-and-incapable-Drunk?-Yes-Six-shillings-move-on-NEXT!' – and then returned to the cell, to listen once more to the talk of the cheerful Cockney malefactors.

But his luck was out as far as prison was concerned. The police decided that a day in custody served for the fine and shot him out into the street with twopence in hand. 'Damnably hungry' he went to the Church Army shelter at 176 Waterloo Road, where a night's sleep and corned beef were exchanged for four hours' work sawing wood, and a prayer meeting.

Discouraged, he went back to Rees's in the morning, got more money and walked north to Edmonton casual ward, where, only slightly drunk this time, he presented himself, hoping this would lead to prison – as indeed under the regulations it should have. But the subworld was rejecting him, for the porter evidently felt 'a tramp with money enough to buy drink ought to be respected'. His luck was running out: during the next few days he tried to tempt fate by begging under the noses of the police. He bore a charmed life and they took no notice. He made no more attempts to put himself the wrong side of bars: by Easter he was in a position of authority himself, wielding a stick as a schoolmaster.

From left to right, 24, 22 and 20 Portobello Road. At number twenty-four Ruth Pitter worked in the studio of the Walberswick Peasant Pottery Co. Ltd., finding Orwell lodgings next door with Mrs Craig. Her neighbour, the jobbing builder to whom she had never spoken, was at number twenty.

Limehouse, London's Chinatown, in 1935.

The Romford workhouse, now part of the Oldchurch hospital, was extensively rebuilt in the late nineteenth century. Its casual ward (arrowed) was the first that Orwell visited. He describes it as 'a grim, smoky yellow cube of brick'. Romford (Orwell calls it 'Romton') was a 'cocoa spike', providing this as opposed to skilly or tea. Tramps were let in at 6 pm, two hours earlier in winter. Often, the morning after their admittance, they were made to break stones; but Orwell and his companions were let out early. On the wall of one of the sleeping cells was inscribed this verse:

'When I was young and in my
    prime
I'd break my stones by dinner
    time,
But now I'm old and getting
    grey
It takes me all the fucking
    day.'

Postcard pictures of Petticoat Lane (Middlesex Street), E1, in the 1930s.

Tramps standing outside a casual ward while the 'tramp major' assigns them tasks.

1b Oakwood Road in Hampstead Garden Suburb, the former home of Mrs Mabel Fierz.

Cockney hop-pickers in Kent in the 1930s.

Tooley Street, SE1. Orwell writes that he lived in a common lodging house here after returning from hop-picking.

Bermondsey public library, Spa Road, SE16; probably where Orwell wrote up his hop-picking experience.

33 Cheyne Walk, SW3: the angled building at the centre of the picture. Orwell used Richard Rees's flat here to change into tramping clothes.

Chelsea casual ward, 47 Milman's Street, SW10. 'Chelsea was said to be the most luxurious spike in England; someone, praising it, said that the blankets there were more like prison than the spike.'

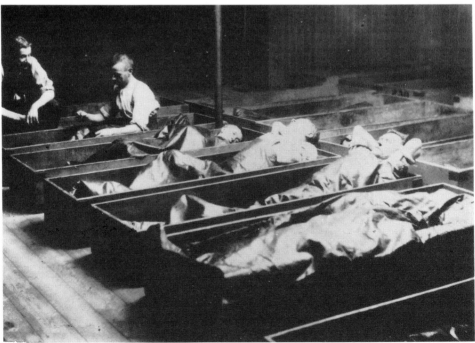

'The Coffin, at fourpence a night. At the Coffin you sleep in a wooden box, with a tarpaulin for covering. It is cold, and the worst thing about it are the bugs, which, being enclosed in a box, you cannot escape.'

A Rowton House, Bondway, Vauxhall, SW8. Montagu Corry, first Baron Rowton, was private secretary to Disraeli until the latter's death in 1881. He was concerned to improve the dwellings of the working classes and conceived the idea of a 'poor man's hotel'. This should offer better accommodation than the common lodging-houses, but at similar prices. The first 'Rowton House', left, cost its originator £30,000, but subsequently they were instituted on a fully commercial basis. Today, neither the exterior nor interior decoration of these monolithic buildings is what it used to be. Orwell writes of the 'excellent bathrooms', and the hotel-like privacy. This house is clamorous and smelly, and not all that cheap at around £15 per week.

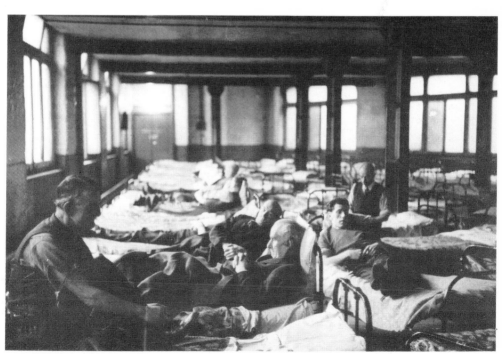

In the dormitory of an East End hostel.

Inside a Salvation Army shelter at sermon-time, during the 1930s. 'To my eye these Salvation Army shelters, though clean, are far drearier than the worst of the common lodging-houses. . . . In some of them there is even a compulsory religious service once or twice a week, which the lodgers must attend or leave the house.'

Century House, Westminster Bridge Road, SE1. The tower block is on the site of one of Lewis Levy's common lodging houses at which Orwell used to stay. Century House represents a change he might have enjoyed, in a gloomy way. It houses MI6.

Billingsgate fish market, EC1. The market's activities are now packed up and transferred to the Isle of Dogs.

Part of the Windsor housing estate off the Harrow Road in Paddington, where Orwell lived for a few months in 1931. A modern estate has now replaced it.

The Waterloo Road and the Cut, SE1, at the centre of Orwell's, and Dorothy's, tramping experiences.

Poplar workhouse, now demolished, in St Leonard's Road, E14. It features in People of the abyss *by Jack London, the greatest single influence on Orwell to become a reporter of low life.*

Inside the Bruce House at Drury Lane, WC2. Orwell thought it excellent value at 1s 1d.

In the cells at Bethnal Green Police Station, 458 Bethnal Green Road, E2. Gordon Comstock behaves much worse at the police station than his author, striking a policeman. Orwell modelled the cells in the Ministry of Love partly on the one he had here, with its board bed and ever-burning light, and like Winston he counted the number of white porcelain bricks in the walls, now painted over.

St Jude's Church, Gray's Inn Road, WC1. Now demolished except for the church hall, this is 'dat dere church in de Gray's Inn Road' that took tramps in on winter nights, referred to by Mrs McElligot in A clergyman's daughter.

On the evening of Tuesday 18th October, 1932, unemployed men marched on the County Hall (completed earlier that year) during a meeting of the LCC. The police intercepted them and in an exchange that lasted four hours there were numerous arrests and twenty-four policemen injured. In Lower Marsh, SE1, next to Waterloo station, mounted police armed with long staves charged from both ends of the street and met in the centre, driving demonstrators into the houses and shops. The police hauled them out and charged them next morning with illegal entry. 'I know the quarter where it happened so well', Orwell wrote to a friend, 'I dare say some of my friends took part in it.'

Inside Old Street Magistrates' Court, EC1.

3

COMING UP FOR AIR

In the summer term of 1932 Orwell became a teacher at a small private school. At the age of twenty-nine his career was a broken one, a mixture of achievement and wilful lapse, as he alternately fulfilled and denied reasonable expectation. From a successful prep school he had gone on a scholarship to Eton, but from there to a post in Burma based on his family's tradition, not his school's, which would have sent him to Oxford or Cambridge. He went on to abandon that job of pensioned, lifelong security for an unpromising and precarious life as a writer, bohemian and beggar. This apostasy he now in turn exchanged for the dowdy respectability of private-school teacher.

It may have been a reluctant act of conformity, a concession to financial necessity, for he had previously resisted Ruth Pitter's urgings to get a job and so relieve his poverty, dismissing the idea as bourgeois. But perhaps, like Gordon Comstock, his attitude to coming back to the surface was ambiguous: he was defeated, but may have been prepared to enjoy a sense of renewal. In fact, unknowingly, he was conforming not merely to middle-class pressure, but also to the pattern established by much of the literary talent of his generation: 'To many an unknown genius postmen bring Typed notices from Rabbitarse and String.' Auden (quoted here), Waugh, Day-Lewis, Warner and Isherwood all in the early stages of their careers taught little boys.

The Hawthorns High School for Boys in Church Road, Hayes, was a day school with only two masters of whom Orwell was one, teaching fifteen or so boys of moderate ability to the age of sixteen. It was an unlikely place for an Old Etonian to be, and the district he found not altogether attractive. Hayes, or nearby Southall, is the setting for George Bowling's suburban confinement in *Coming up for air*, and aspects of it are blended with Southwold to produce Knype Hill in *A clergyman's daughter*, where Dorothy Hare lives in penurious servitude. 'The most disagreeable thing here', he wrote in June 1932, 'is not the job itself (it is a day school, thank God, so I have nothing to do with the brats out of school hours) but Hayes itself, which is one of the most godforsaken places I have ever struck. The population seems to be entirely made up of clerks who frequent tin-roofed chapels on Sundays & for the rest bolt themselves within doors.'

The period between the wars saw a massive expansion of London's western industrial suburbs. In Southall and Hayes, chemical works, steam flour-mills, a margarine factory and long cloned rows of small newly-built redbrick houses coexisted with what once were rural communities. A few minutes' walk down the hill from the thirteenth century Hayes parish church and village pond were the factories of His Master's Voice and the Aeolian Musical Instrument Company. George Bowling is one of the invaders, but a reluctant one:

Do you know the road I live in – Ellesmere Road, West Bletchley? Even if you don't, you know fifty others exactly like it.

You know how these streets fester all over the inner-outer suburbs. Always the same. Long, long rows of little semi-detached houses – the numbers in Ellesmere Road run to 212 and ours is 191 – as much alike as council houses and generally uglier. The stucco front, the creosoted gate, the privet hedge, the green front door. The Laurels, the Myrtles, the Hawthorns, Mon Abri, Mon Repos, Belle Vue. At perhaps one house in fifty some anti-social type who'll probably end in the workhouse has painted his front door blue instead of green.

If it was godforsaken and parvenu, Orwell did his best to centre his life there on traditional values. He made friends with the local curate and his wife and attended the parish's High Anglian mass regularly, perhaps more from a sense of contact with an English tradition than from religious belief. He gardened too, did some fishing, and occupied himself and his boys in nature study, going birds'-nesting, keeping a pickle-jar aquarium – 'we have newts, tadpoles, caddis-flies etc' – and collecting moth eggs and marsh gas from nearby Cranford Parkway. He seems to have been a popular teacher, though a little idiosyncratic, a pupil remembers:

He had a dual personality, because he would cane you unmercifully at the slightest provocation, but could be kindness itself to those who showed interest in what he was interested in.

He was very much an introvert. He would sit at his desk and start smiling and no-one knew what he was laughing at. He was aware that this was strange, so if it happened at mealtimes, he would turn round and feed the proprietor's parrot to hide his face.

Orwell later wrote, 'I notice that many people never laugh when they [think they] are alone, and I suppose that if a man does not laugh when he is alone his inner life must be relatively barren.'

The retreat into an inner life typifies his relationship with Hayes; it was an open prison from which he continually sought escape: in correspondences and relationships with women; train journeys into the country for walks; trips to the centre of London, fifteen miles away, for theatre productions and to complete his fieldwork on the roofless. Transfer rather than escape came after four terms at the Hawthorns. The school, pupils and staff, was taken over by a much larger outfit with a boarding house, called Frays College, in the Harefield Road in nearby Uxbridge. Orwell moved there for the winter term of 1933 – but not for long, for in December he almost died of pneumonia.

He had bought a motorbicycle and made it his habit, even in the wintertime, to ride it wearing only bags and a sports-jacket. In the middle of December he returned to Frays blue with cold and drenched by the rain. He caught a chill, and at first the school matron and the headmaster's wife cared for him. But soon he developed pneumonia and had to be moved, fatally ill, it was thought, up the Harefield Road to Uxbridge Cottage Hospital. When his mother and sister arrived the crisis had passed, and he was recovering; but Avril was told he had been in a state of delirium and distress:

he'd been talking the whole time about money. We reassured him that everything was all right, and he needn't worry about money. It turned out that it wasn't actually his situation in life as regards money that he was worrying about but it was actual cash: he felt that he wanted cash sort of under his pillow.

A few years before, in a lodging house near the Strand, he had woken up around midnight to find a man trying to steal money from him. 'He was pretending to be asleep while he did it, sliding his hand under the pillow as gently as a rat.'

So weak was his constitution and so severe his illness that on doctor's orders he was forbidden to teach for six months. In fact, he was not to return to teaching at all – it had never been his vocation. He left the hospital in early January 1934, spent a few days in an Ealing hotel to recover strength enough to travel, and then went back, again, to Southwold. He stayed there more than six months, in fact until November, using the time to write *A clergyman's daughter*.

The Hawthorns School for Boys, 116 Church Road, Hayes, Middlesex. At one stage of its history the Hayes rectory and now a small hotel, The Hawthorns became a school after the First World War. The school was the left-hand side of the building.

Madonna and child, St Mary the Virgin, Hayes. This is the 'quite skittish-looking BVM, half life-size' which Orwell undertook to repaint, first using onion water to clean it. He tried to make her look 'as much like one of the illustrations in La Vie Parisienne *as possible'.*

She has been moved from the southern to the northern side of the nave since Orwell's time, and, alas, has been redecorated.

The Parish Church of St Mary the Virgin, Church Road, Hayes, Middlesex. This, John Betjeman said, is 'one of the gems of Middlesex'; certainly, preserved in part from the thirteenth-century amidst the recent development, it is a lovingly tended church, with a sixteenth-century lych gate and fifteenth-century mural of St Christopher. There is a High Church tradition here and Orwell complained at first that 'the service is so popish that I don't know my way about it & feel an awful BF when I see everyone bowing & crossing themselves all around me & can't follow suit.' The rector in Orwell's time was Ernest Hudson, a man coming to the end of his career in the church. He seems to be a partial prototype for the Reverend Hare of Knype Hill. Orwell suspected they both hated being dressed up in the High Anglican fashion and led round in procession 'like a bullock garlanded for sacrifice'. The gruesome Miss Mayfill of the same novel has her original here, 'a moribund hag who stinks of mothballs and gin, & has to be more or less carried to & from the altar at communion'. One can imagine Orwell, like Dorothy, praying to get to the chalice before she does, to avoid the imprint of her large, loose lips.

The His Master's Voice (Thorn EMI) gramophone factory, Hayes. Orwell's poem, 'On a ruined farm near the His Master's Voice gramophone factory' was carried in the Adelphi *of April 1934. It was written at the time when the new Hayes was still under construction, giving him a feeling of discontinuity and dislocation:*

There is my world, my home; yet why

So alien still?

Macbeth *at the Old Vic, Waterloo Road, SE1. Orwell went to see this production, which had Margaret Webster playing opposite Malcolm Keen, in November, 1932, with his friend Eleanor Jaques. 'I so adore* Macbeth*', he wrote to her. In June 1940, he went back there to review* The Tempest *for* Time and Tide*: 'If there really is such a thing as turning in one's grave, Shakespeare must get a lot of exercise . . . Nine-tenths of the people watching don't know the text and can be counted on to miss the point of any joke that is not followed up by a kick on the buttocks.'*

Frays College, 65 Harefield Road, Uxbridge. The house dates from about 1860, but was bought in 1926 by a small-scale educational reformer, John Bennett. It was named after the adjacent Frays River, and took both boys and girls. Orwell wasn't impressed with his first viewing in July 1933: 'I went over to see the prize-giving at the school & it looked pretty bloody – the girls' section of the school (which I shall have nothing to do with – perhaps it is for the best) sang the female version of Kipling's "If".'
The school closed in 1974, but reopened the following year as an Adult Education Centre.

Uxbridge Cottage Hospital, Harefield Road, Uxbridge. This small 1920s nursing hospital, where Orwell was brought with the attack of pneumonia which cut short hi teaching career, is at the northern end of Harefield Road. It is now deserted.

4

ON THE FRONTIER

In the last quarter of 1934 Orwell left his parents' home for the last time and moved to Hampstead, the most assertively picturesque of the London villages; though its community pretends to be nonchalantly inattentive to an ambience of Keats, Constable and cobblestones. For Orwell it was another period on the fringe – of central London, of the Heath, and of literary life. Like Paris though, and unlike Bermondsey and Uxbridge, it was one of the more fashionable, bohemian fringes, mocked or despised in his writings, but, in practice, endured with surprising good grace.

Through his Esperanto-speaking Aunt Nellie (who had sent him six shillings for Christmas in 1918) Orwell had got an afternoon job in a secondhand bookshop called Booklovers' Corner, on South End Green, where he could live and write above the premises in the mornings and evenings. Without doubt he was now an author. *Down and out in Paris and London* and *Burmese days* were published, *A clergyman's daughter* submitted. *Keep the aspidistra flying* was in the process of being written and, indeed, experienced.

Booklovers' Corner was to become Mr McKechnie's bookshop where Gordon Comstock works with inward spleen and outward servility, rationing his cigarettes and waiting for the apocalypse. It seems to have been a dualism faithful to life, because his fellow assistant Jon Kimche, who worked the mornings, recalls how in their sitting room in the evenings 'Orwell would at times hold forth in long harangues against the smooth literary young men from Cambridge who had everything going for them, or else against the British Empire, the Catholic Church, or the filthy rich.' In the shop, a customer remembers, Orwell was uniformly polite, helpful and informative.

'Our shop', Orwell later wrote, 'stood exactly on the frontier between Hampstead and Camden Town, and we were frequented by all types from baronets to bus-conductors.' Further, it had 'an exceptionally interesting stock' and, while he may have been underpaid, he was certainly not overworked; looking back on 'my employer's kindness to me, and some happy days I spent in the shop' he found it a congenial life if not one to which he would return. The shop not only sold books, but was a twopenny fiction library, and moreover was stocked with various sidelines:

We sold second-hand typewriters, for instance, also stamps – used stamps I mean. . . . At Christmas time we spent a feverish ten days struggling with Christmas cards and calendars, which are tiresome things to sell but good business while the season lasts. It used to interest me to see the brutal cynicism with which Christian sentiment is exploited. The touts from the Christmas card firms used to come round with their catalogues as early as June. A phrase from one of their invoices sticks in my memory. It was: '2 doz. Infant Jesus with rabbits'.

Kimche remembers Orwell standing at the front of the shop selling stamps: 'Tall and gaunt, looking straight ahead of him, as he always did in argument, he is holding forth to a very small boy about the value of a foreign stamp. Far below, the boy, not at all overawed, keeps up his end of the argument as to why he should have the stamp for a penny or two less.'

In February 1935 Orwell learned that he could not keep his room above the bookshop, but had to move. The remarkable, indefatigable Mabel Fierz found a room for him at 77 Parliament Hill, next to the open space of Hampstead Heath; she had his weak lungs in mind. She seems secretly to have paid part of his rent. In early March he wrote to a woman friend to protest his independence there, and domestication:

No, I *don't* feed entirely on things that don't need cooking. I have bought a small gas-stove called a Bachelor Griller, and you can grill, boil and fry on it, but not bake. As a matter of fact I can cook not too badly, and I have already given a dinner-party to three people all at once and cooked everything myself.

The three people invited were a current girlfriend and Rayner Heppenstall and Michael Sayers. Heppenstall remembered they drank beer and that Orwell cooked 'very good steak', and he thought too that the girlfriend was an improvement: 'Eric's new girl was as plain as the old one but of a livelier and more attractive personality. Indeed, "plain" is not quite the word. The last girl had been of a more or less average size and shape, mouse-coloured and bespectacled, with a squint and a stoop.' Connolly was invited once as well – the first time they had met for almost fifteen years. Orwell's greeting was 'typical, a long but not unfriendly stare and his characteristic wheezy laugh,

"Well Connolly, I can see that you've worn a good deal better than I have".' Connolly was dumbstruck, altogether unprepared for the ravaged look of Orwell's previously pear-shaped face.

A little later that year Orwell was to meet the girl who became his wife. He asked his landlady, a graduate psychologist at University College in Gower Street, if they might give a joint party. They did, he inviting Richard Rees, she among others a fellow student, Eileen O'Shaughnessy. A friend described her in this way: 'Small with blue eyes and nearly black hair. Pretty, with very pretty hands and feet and body beautifully poised on her legs. Good but shabby and unbrushed clothes, generally black. She generally walked as if she wasn't thinking where she was going, as indeed she seldom was.' Gangling and awkward, unsure of women but urgently persistent with them, Orwell left off leaning on the mantelpiece, and paid attention to Eileen that evening. He would have been wearing his baggy grey flannel trousers and leather-elbowed sports-jacket, with dark shirt and pale, hairy tie. She remembered later that she was 'rather drunk and behaving my worst, very rowdy'. When the evening came to an end he walked the guests down the hill to South End Green, returning to say, 'Now *that* is the kind of girl I would like to marry!' They had dinner the next week and Orwell again walked her down to her train. A few weeks later she met her friend, the author and translator, Elisaveta Fen:

Eileen told me that she had met Orwell again and that he as good as proposed to her. 'What! already?' I exclaimed. 'What did he say?'
'He said he wasn't really eligible but . . .'
'And what did you reply?'
'Nothing . . . I just let him talk on.'
'What are you going to do about it?'
'I don't know . . . You see, I told myself that when I was thirty I would accept the first man who asked me to marry him. Well . . . I shall be thirty next year. . . .'

In August 1935 Orwell removed again, and once more through Mabel Fierz's agency. He went to 50 Lawford Road in Kentish Town, some minutes' walk from his work, this time to form a menage with Heppenstall, whom he thought 'very nice', and Sayers. They were at the top of the house which dated from the 1860s, a tram-driver and a plumber and their wives below them. Heppenstall recalls the living arrangements: 'We had three rooms, a kitchen and a lavatory, compactly disposed. One of the two rooms at the front was very small, a mere boxroom. I, able to pay least rent, had this. Michael had the other front room, but seemed likely to spend little time in it. Eric had the big room at the back. In it, all eating was done at a big scrubbed table.' Sayers was indeed seldom there and, Auden-like, Orwell established the rhythms and disciplines of the house. Heppenstall loafed around undressed and unshaven before going out to watch ballet and drink. Orwell rose first in the mornings, made breakfast, sometimes with 'gravy dips' (these were spoonfuls of flour paste dropped into the hot fat in a frying pan), and called Heppenstall to come and eat it. His duties were confined to such tasks as bending the dinner spaghetti into pans of boiling water and fetching beer from down the road. But it was always himself, Heppenstall noticed, who had to unscrew the difficult bottle-stoppers and jar-lids: 'There was a curious lack of strength in that tall, raw-boned frame.' Once there were two visitors: Orwell's sister Avril and friend Brenda Salkeld turned up together.

Sometimes Orwell would tell his housemate anecdotes about being an author. One was that Gollancz meddled with the lines of reviews used for promotion: 'so that, for instance, if a reviewer said, "This is by no means a masterpiece", the statement would appear on a jacket as, "This is . . . a masterpiece".'

Another of Orwell's jokes was about replying to American woman readers of one's books. They always, said Eric, sent him a questionnaire, and the first question would be, 'What do you consider the most worthwhile thing in life?' To this, said Eric, he always replied, 'The love of a good woman'.

Heppenstall wondered just how many questionnaires Orwell had received from American women readers.

Unknown to Heppenstall, Orwell's good feeling for him was wearing thin. One night the ballet critic came home drunk and was lectured for his irresponsibility: 'Bit thick, you know . . . This time of night . . . Wake up the whole street . . . I can put up with a lot . . . A bit of consideration . . . After all . . .' Heppenstall got up to protest, physically, and Orwell knocked him out. When he came to, he tottered off to bed, but then Orwell came down the passage and locked the bedroom door. Heppenstall was sufficiently roused to indignation to get up and begin kicking down the door, whereupon he found himself again confronted by Orwell – this time armed with a shooting stick. He poked Heppenstall in the stomach with this and he cracked him over the legs, before aiming a more serious blow from aloft which Heppenstall parried with a chair. Then Orwell retired, perhaps when the tram-driver and plumber appeared. They took the victim downstairs for a cup of tea. 'We never did think much of that Mr Blair', said the tram-driver's wife. 'Keeps us awake till three and four o'clock in the morning he does sometimes with his typing.'

In the morning Heppenstall was summoned into Orwell's room. 'He sat there and interviewed me like a district commissioner.' Heppenstall was turned out.

By January 1936, with his third book published, and his fourth written and submitted, Orwell had used, used up, all his adult experience. Burma, Paris, tramping in London, hop-picking, school-teaching, bookselling – they had all been put to use. Even his forth-coming marriage was anticipated in the last pages of his latest type-script. It is hard to conceive what kind of reworking or imaginative leap he would have found possible had a book not been commissioned from him. But Victor Gollancz asked Orwell to write about the impact of the depression on the north of England. The advance was good and he accepted. He left Lawford Road, Booklovers' Corner and London and would not return to live there for over four years. They were years of importance. In them he became a married man and a well-known writer. He became politically educated and politically passionate. He lived in the squalor of the industrial north and in rural retreat in Hertfordshire. He fought and nearly died in Spain, and came back almost overcome with a sense of crisis. It was to face that crisis that he returned to London in 1940, to be at the heart of a saving socialist revolution and, just as urgently perhaps, to respond to his own taunt from his childhood:

> Awake! Oh you young men of England
> For if when your country's in need
> You do not enlist by the thousand
> You truly are cowards indeed.

Booklovers' Corner, South End Green, NW3. The bookshop, described by one customer as 'a gloomy cave of a place', was until recently, but after Orwell's time, the Prompt Corner, a chess-players' cafe. Now it is a pizza house.

77 Parliament Hill, NW3. Orwell's room, apparently very untidy and with mice nesting in a spare blanket, was on the first floor and looking out over the back.

(above)
40 Well Walk, NW3. A former home of the painter Constable. In the 1930s a forgettable poet called T. Sturge Moore lived here, penning such lines as 'Quit the earth and climb a cloud!' He held 'Friday Evenings at Home', poetic occasions which Orwell attended. Once he brought his mother along, but she went to sleep.

50 Lawford Road, NW5, Orwell's home from August 1935 to January 1936.

The Duke of Cambridge, Bartholomew Road, NW5. The 1860s public house at the end of Lawford Road where Heppenstall went, jug in hand, to get in the evening's beer.

St Pancras public bath and washhouses, Prince of Wales Road, NW5. These were built with great style in 1901. Orwell visited them weekly. Heppenstall avoided their rigours and went instead to the Fierzes'.

5

BACK FOR THE BLITZ

Some quiet morning, when the clerks are streaming across London Bridge, and the canary's singing and the old woman's pegging the bloomers on the line – zoom, whizz, plonk! Houses going up into the air, bloomers soaked with blood, canary singing on above the corpses. (*Coming up for air*)

In the event, the informed estimates through the 1930s of the devastation to be made on London by German bombing planes were mistaken. Both the populace, a quarter of which fled the city, and the government, which stockpiled cardboard coffins, expected far worse. Orwell and his wife were safe in the country when war broke out, in just the kind of location the 'bomb-dodgers' favoured. Yet they left their sweetshop cottage and returned to London. After the move he explained why to Julian Symons:

He hated cities, he said, they were dirty, foul, self-destroying. 'But you've got to stay here while the war's on. You can't leave when people are being bombed to hell.' My own feelings were so unheroically opposite to these that I goggled at him. But he was perfectly serious. He had lived in the country before the war, he said, and when it was over he and his wife would live there again, but in the meantime it was necessary to stay in London, to set an example.

Eileen set the example first, moving to her family's home in Greenwich and a job with the Censorship Department. She went, a friend thought, because she felt 'it would be wrong for her to stay in a safe place while the rest of her family was exposed to the danger of air-raids.' Her family was at 24 Croom's Hill, a handsome, bow-fronted, seventeenth-century house. Living in Hertfordshire, the Orwells had stayed there often when visiting London. Croom's Hill borders on Greenwich Park, and Orwell later wrote of walking to the top of the hill and having 'the mild thrill of standing exactly on longitude 0°'. From there, he went on, you could examine Greenwich Observatory, 'the ugliest building in the world', and marvel that its architects could have designed it so when they had Wren's Hospital and Inigo Jones's Queen's House beneath their very eyes.

Meanwhile, he wrote on into 1940 in the country, though at the same time making efforts to join the army, or at least to join in the wartime activity in some way. The army didn't want him, not did anybody: 'Like nearly everyone else I have completely failed to get any kind of "war work". But I am trying very hard to join a Govt training centre & learn machine draughtmanship'. He wanted to prepare his hands for post-revolution England. Only *Time and Tide*, a lightweight middle-brow journal, was prepared to offer him work, hardly war work though: theatre reviewing. He took it on, moving to London in May 1940.

He and Eileen rented a flat near Baker Street, at 18 Dorset Chambers in Chagford Street. It was at the top of the house and so especially dangerous, but they faced hostilities with a sense of adventure. 'Whenever the sirens let out their warning wail,' Elisaveta Fen remembers, 'Eileen would put out the lights in their top floor flat, open the windows and watch the happenings in the street. I do not think she ever used an air-raid shelter herself, and instead of using the cottage at Wallington as a safe hide-out, or even as a place of rest, she and George decided to give it up altogether just when the air-raids got under weigh, in October 1940.'

Orwell was writing uninspired theatre criticism, but the war he found greatly exciting. 'Constantly, as I walk down the street, I find myself looking up at the windows to see which of them would make good machine-gun nests.' Writing his diary became an act of daring, walking home an exploration: 'Almost impossible to write in this infernal racket. (Electric lights have just gone off. Luckily I have some candles.) So many streets in (lights on again) the quarter roped off because of unexploded bombs, that to get home from Baker Street, say three hundred yards, is like trying to find your way to the heart of a maze.' 'He felt enormously at home in the Blitz,' Connolly thought, 'among the bombs, the bravery, the rubble, the shortages, the homeless, the signs of rising revolutionary temper.' Particularly he interested himself in the phenomenon of Tube shelterers. In November 1940 it was estimated that 200,000 people were using the Underground to shelter from bombs, and he had heard that Jews made a particular use of it. 'Must try and verify this', he noted. He did, at the Chancery Lane, Oxford Circus and Baker Street stations: '*Not* all Jews, but, I think, a higher proportion of Jews than one would normally see in a crowd of this size.'

On 14th May 1940 the Local Defence Volunteers was formed, soon
to be reformed as the Home Guard, and Orwell joined the St John's
Wood company within a month. He accepted the rank of sergeant, con-
ferred because of his experience of war in Spain, but was never to
become an officer. The ranks of the Home Guard, he hoped, were to be
a force in the coming socialist uprising; the gutters would run with
blood and red guards would billet in the Ritz. This revolutionary
promise, born as in Spain of an armed and disillusioned populace, was
his consolation for not being able to fight fascism directly. It was an
insufficient rationalisation as he revealed when, through Mark
Benney, the possibility arose of him working in a 'hush-hush section of
the RAF'. A resplendent squadron leader, Alan Clutton-Brock, came
round to Chagford Street and took his part in a bizarre and unfruitful
dialogue:

'I can't say anything about the work, of course, but I assure you it's tedious
beyond belief. And the dreadful people you meet!'

'I wouldn't want a commission, you understand. I'd be quite happy in the
ranks.'

'And you have to do six weeks of foot-training first – insufferable! In fact,
until it occurred to me to think of the whole thing as a kind of ballet I didn't
think I'd survive it!'

'But I like drills. I know the Manual by heart. I need the discipline!'

He was both wistful and angry that his country wouldn't allow him
to shoot fascists. When he heard Evelyn Waugh was serving with a
Commando unit he asked Anthony Powell, 'Why can't somebody on
the Left do that sort of thing?' But for his ill-health he would certainly
have done it. 'I hold what half the men in this country would give their
balls to have', he used to tell William Empson, meaning the card
exempting him from conscription: 'The impudence of it, when they
know perfectly well I'm too ill to stay here. Probably save my life to go
to North Africa. But if it didn't, they might have to give the widow
something, d'you see.'

After almost a year in Chagford Street the Orwells moved out to St
John's Wood, and the fifth floor of a large, and presently well-
appointed, block of flats off the Abbey Road, 111 Langford Court – at
this time full of refugees. As was his practice, Orwell turned one room
into a workshop and set about making bookshelves. Mark Benney went
round to see him one Sunday afternoon when they were just getting
settled down, and helped him stack his books on the newly-made
shelves:

There was an air-raid warning and somewhere, perhaps a mile away, a bomb fell. The slight jar of the shock-waves brought his new bookshelves and his books clattering to the floor, and since nothing else in the apartment was disturbed, it was clearly his handiwork, and not the enemy, that was to blame; but he was surprisingly morose when we pointed this out.

H. G. Wells came to dinner there on one memorable occasion and, according to one account, so greedily ate the curry and the fruitcake Eileen had made that he was taken ill, and the taxi taking him home had to rush him to hospital instead.

The Orwells clearly were looking out for a pleasanter flat than Langford Court, high up as it was and full of foreigners. In the summer of 1942 they found one, moving to 10a Mortimer Crescent, the lower half of a semi-detached house of about 1850, a short walk north up the Abbey Road. Anthony Powell says its Victorianism delighted Orwell:

The house conjured up those middle-to-lower-middle-class households . . . on which his mind loved to dwell. . . . 'They would probably have kept a Buttons here.' he said, enchanted at the thought. . . . The sitting-room, with a background of furniture dating from more prosperous generations of bygone Blairs, two or three 18th century family portraits hanging on the walls, might well have been in the owner's study in a country house.

Not everyone thought it so wonderful as Orwell. 'A remarkably dreary flat', 'an icily cold flat', 'a damp basement flat' are other memories. Certainly it must have been a spartan place to wake up in on a winter morning, because the boiler went out if someone didn't get up to stoke it in the night. Ruth Pitter has a memory of an evening she spent there:

While we were talking, and working away at cooking supper (I remember part of it was apple-pie, and [Eileen] was nervously anxious not to leave a scrap of core in the apples, as she said he disliked it so) – while we were working and talking, Orwell came in. Like a ghost. . . . The emaciation, the waxen pallor, the slow, careful movements, all shocked and distressed me. But he seemed cheerful, fetched some beer, and went out again to see if his mother would come in – she was living close by. I had brought with me two things impossible to buy in London at that time – a good bunch of grapes from my mother's home in Essex, and a red rose – two rare treasures. I can see him now, holding up the grapes with a smile of admiration and delight on his ravaged face, and then, cupping the rose in his wasted hands, breathing in the scent with a kind of reverent joy.

Pale and exhausted, Orwell was overworking. In 1941 he had at last found 'war work': producing propaganda for the Far East from the bowels of the British Broadcasting Corporation.

24 Croom's Hill, Greenwich, SE10. The home of Eileen's beloved brother Eric and his mother and wife. Eileen came from Hertfordshire to live here before her husband's return to London.

Eileen Blair holding her young nephew Laurence O'Shaughnessy aloft in the back garden of Croom's Hill. The picture was taken in 1939.

The crypt of the Parish Church of St Alfege, Greenwich High Road, SE10. Hawksmoor's St Alfege's was built in 1714. During World War II the crypt was used as a bomb-shelter by Orwell and other locals, holding up to 250 people. When full, the stench of live bodies, he was told, was 'almost insupportable'. But he had a more deep-seated horror of such places, which made for a family dispute, he obstinately arguing that it was far worse for the children there to be playing among vaults full of corpses than that they should have to put up with the stink of the living. The church was burnt out by a German incendiary bomb in March 1941, but has been faithfully refurbished.

Dorset Chambers, Chagford Street, NW1. The Blairs lived here at number eighteen from May 1940 to April 1941.

Bloomsbury Street, WC1. Here on the eastern side were Lady Rhondda's Time and Tide *offices at number thirty-eight. Orwell must have known the street well, because Richard Rees's* Adelphi, *with which he effectively began his journalistic career, was at number fifty-two.*

Sir Stephen Spender at the former Horizon *offices, 6 Selwyn House, Lansdowne Terrace, WC1. Much of Orwell's best journalism was written for* Horizon, *edited by Cyril Connolly, assisted for a time by Spender. Spender lived on the job, and on one occasion Orwell stayed the night, sleeping through the noise of the anti-aircraft battery firing night-long in Brunswick Square.*

Soldiers evacuated from Dunkirk arriving in London on 31st May, 1940. 1st June, 1940: 'Last night to Waterloo and Victoria to see whether I could get any news of E. Quite impossible, of course.' Orwell was looking for Eric O'Shaughnessy, Eileen's brother, who had in fact been killed in the evacuation. It was a blow from which Eileen took years to recover.

Workmen taking iron railings for scrap from a North London house. Orwell always understood the wartime removal of iron railings from London's parks and squares to be a democratic gesture and not just a source of scrap iron for the war effort. It was an understanding suggested perhaps by a letter of Margot Asquith to the Times, 15th October 1940:

'I think the Government should make up its mind whether it wants scrap iron or whether it has enough. I should have thought it was a golden opportunity to rid our London squares of their ugly iron railings. I have lived for many years in Bedford Square and can truly say that I have never seen anyone in it. The removal of all the railings in Hyde Park is an acknowledged improvement.

'Why should we not do the same in our fettered and deserted squares? There are many poor people in my neighbourhood, and elsewhere, who might enjoy sitting under the lovely trees of most of our London squares. It is the height of selfishness to deny them this innocent pleasure. In no other city of Europe that I know of does the same selfishness prevail.'

A bombed graveyard in South London. Orwell noted in his diary that he dreaded the consequences of such an event.

A detail from the dogs' cemetery in Kensington Gardens, near Lancaster Gate, W2. Among 'the most horrible spectacles in England', Orwell judged.

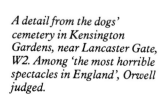

'And the large families one sees here and there, father, mother, and several children all laid out in a row like rabbits on the slab. They all seem so peacefully asleep in the bright lamplight. The children lying on their backs, with their little pink cheeks like wax dolls, and all fast asleep.'

(below)
London Docks burning after the first daylight mass raid on London, 7th September, 1940. Orwell was one of Cyril Connolly's guests for tea on the afternoon of this raid, at his top-floor flat at 49 Bedford Square, WC1. 'The only person suitably impressed was Connolly, who took us up on the roof and, after gazing for some time at the fires, said "It's the end of capitalism. It's a judgement on us." I didn't feel this to be so, but was chiefly struck by the size and beauty of the flames.'

The Osterley Park School for Home Guards at Isleworth in Middlesex, opened by Spanish Civil War veteran Tom Wintringham on 15th July, 1940, ran until October that year, when it was taken over by the War Office. The Home Guard training was then moved elsewhere, owing to the difficulties at Osterley of providing sufficient winter accommodation. Orwell was one of 4,940 men to attend the free two-day course, writing enthusiastically about it in Horizon in 1941. Instruction was given in static defence and guerrilla warfare, stalking and scoutcraft, defence against parachutists, and such skills as the decapitation of enemy motorcyclists with trip-wire. There was an improvised and imaginative quality to the training, based largely on experiences with the International Brigade. After Dunkirk, the overwhelming invasion threat was thought to be the tank, and Osterley set out to 'debunk the tank' by means of irregular tactics.

Three Spaniards taught the use of Molotov cocktails to destroy Panzer divisions. The Park and Osterley House, a fine Adam mansion, are open to the public.

Drill Hall, Allitsen Road, NW8. It was at this hall, now used by the U.S. Marines who guard their ambassador's residence in Regent's Park, that Sergeant Blair ferociously prepared his recruits for action. He was enthusiastic but, Fredric Warburg who was a corporal under Orwell says, not altogether competent. Doing mortar drill in a garage off the Edgware Road he inadvertently had a live, but unexplosive, shell loaded into an unsecured mortar. When fired the shell narrowly failed to decapitate one guard, while the gun itself recoiled into two privates' faces. The consequent court of inquiry took no disciplinary action on the sergeant, but awarded one of the soldiers around £100, to pay for a set of dentures, a sum which, Warburg remembered, 'appeared to Orwell altogether excessive'.

111 Langford Court, Langford Place, NW8. Orwell and Eileen lived here from 1941–42. In May 1941, when they had just moved in, a bomb hit the Langford Court garage, causing alarm for the safety of the building itself. The Orwells were temporarily evacuated to the caretaker's room, where they shared some chocolate they had long been saving.

Mortimer Crescent, NW6. 10 Mortimer Crescent no longer exists – Orwell was bombed out – but the nature of the house is reproduced by those original houses remaining.

A 'Second Front' meeting, Trafalgar Square, SW1, 26th July, 1942. There were meetings of tens of thousands of people in Trafalgar Square in 1942 to agitate for a second front against Germany. Orwell probably had these in mind as prototypes for the mass meetings in Victory Square. This is also the place of execution for criminals and prisoners of war in Nineteen eighty-four. *The German wireless, Orwell had noted, urged Londoners to hang Churchill in Trafalgar Square.*

Bedford College, Regent's Park, NW1. The college was evacuated during the war and used as an emergency training school for BBC employees, Orwell among them. 'The Liars' School' it was sometimes called.

6

TALKING TO INDIA

With the outbreak of war there was an urgent need for the foreign services of the BBC to expand, to put the British case to enemies and allies alike. There was a sudden boom in jobs there and Orwell was taken on, not just for his journalistic ability, but more specifically for his experience of the Far East in Burma. He was offered a contract as a Talks Producer on 18th August, 1941, and reported for duty on Monday 25th. He went first of all on his six week course at the 'Liars' School' and began work a little later that year.

The BBC's expansion meant a temporary growth of premises. Under a wartime provision the eastern block of the Peter Robinson department store at 200 Oxford Street and part of the western basement area were requisitioned. It was here that the Eastern Services were to be housed. Orwell found the atmosphere of the BBC 'somewhere halfway between a girls' school and a lunatic asylum', and there was from the beginning a sense of manically disorganised activity about the Oxford Street building. It was due to become operational on 15th March 1942, but when news of this got about among the producers, there was in-fighting and counter-claiming as to who should use which of its facilities. The target date was not kept, and in April the building was still 'badly contractor-ridden'. Internal memos were flying around – for instance, should the scruffy floors be wax-polished? (On the other hand, ought the studios to look resplendent in wartime?)

By 1st June everything seemed ready. But within twenty-four hours cries went up from producers for carpeting, microphone booms, green cue lights and (astonishingly unprovided) clocks. Almost immediately a House Committee was set up to help order the chaos. The basin plugholes of the ladies' washrooms were being clogged up with hair: there should be a notice forbidding the ladies to comb their hair over them, it was suggested. But if the mirrors were removed elsewhere they wouldn't be able to. From the gentlemen's cloakrooms there were complaints that the liquid soap dispensers were filled so full that it was difficult to extract soap from them. This, the committee revealed, was policy: 'to conserve our supplies of liquid soap'. It reported in July that the lifts were unreliable and, what was more, the lift attendants talked too much. The staff as a whole was not talking as quietly as it might – indeed, noise was a great problem.

Orwell was working in an office on the second floor, but only a makeshift one like all the others, for the great high-ceilinged departments were merely partitioned into cubicles, and because of rationing the lath and plaster walls were only just over head high. All sorts of measures had to be introduced to keep down the noise: producers were to sit *next* to their secretaries when dictating, not opposite; the telephones were to be muted, but only when the GPO could get round to it. The constant background of 'conversation, dictation, clattering typewriters and, owing to the shortage of studios, even the rehearsal of talks and features in various oriental languages' annoyed Orwell, as John Morris, later to become head of the Third Programme, has recorded:

It was difficult and at times impossible to carry on a telephone conversation, and my earliest recollection of Orwell is of him standing, with that curiously crucified expression which seemed never to leave his face, in the aperture (there was no door) which separated his room from mine. 'For God's sake shut up,' he would say in his rather harshly petulant voice, and then return to his telephoning. Sometimes he would come back a little later; he would never apologise for his outburst, but as though to hint that he bore no ill-will, would offer me one of the horrible cigarettes which he himself made from a particularly pungent and acrid shag. I would take a puff or two and then, because it started a paroxysm of coughing, would stub out the beastly thing. This would always cause Orwell to smile in a rather contemptuous manner.

William Empson was also on the other side of a partition from Orwell and he sometimes heard him rehearsing a talk with a guest speaker:

At first the visitor would do most of the talking, with George increasing his proportion gradually; no doubt he had to lure the visitor into providing an entry for the tremendous remark which one learned to expect towards the end of the interview. 'The FACK that you're black,' he would say, in a leisurely but somehow exasperated manner, immensely carrying, and all the more officer-class for being souped up into his formalized Cockney, 'and that I'm white, has *nudding whatever to do wiv it.*' I never once heard an Indian say 'But I'm not black', though they must all have wanted to.

Eileen had taken work in Whitehall in 1939, in the Censorship Department. After nearly three years there she switched to the Ministry of Food. She was in Portman Square – sometimes, when

Orwell was ill, having to race back to Mortimer Crescent at mid-day to prepare his lunch. Presumably on his recommendation, she was approached by the producer of a programme for India, 'In Your Kitchen'. In late 1942 she contributed recipes for pancakes, fritters, scones and biscuits – so successfully that she was called upon again for salads, soups and pies.

Both husband and wife, neither constitutionally strong, were being taxed by overwork, and Orwell, ever bronchitic, was in poor health. Laurence Brander, also working at the BBC, met him one winter morning in Portland Place, Orwell wrapped up against the cold to the point of disguise: 'I saw a long way off a very tall figure proceeding towards me. Gradually I made out a pair of gumboots, a huge trench coat, enormous gauntlet gloves and the longest woollen scarf I had ever seen. No hat. Gradually this figure became George Orwell.' The Eastern Service Director at the BBC noted 'the protracted absence of Mr Blair on sick leave'. There were long and irregular hours to be done.

Everyone in the Records Department worked eighteen hours in the twenty-four, with two three-hour snatches of sleep. Mattresses were brought up from the cellars and pitched all over the corridors: meals consisted of sandwiches and Victory Coffee wheeled round on trolleys by attendants from the canteen.

Only the Victory Coffee identifies this as a passage from *Nineteen eighty-four*. BBC workers often had to sleep on the job; in the concert hall at Broadcasting House a night-watchman tiptoed in and out to make sure that Reith's morals were being observed.

The Ministry of Truth is quite evidently based on the wartime BBC. The 'long windowless hall' of the Records Department, 'with its double row of cubicles and its endless rustle of papers and hum of voices' belongs to 200 Oxford Street; so does the canteen, greasy, overcrowded and grimy, with a sour smell of 'bad coffee and metallic stew and dirty clothes'. In fact the canteen, on the ground floor of 200 Oxford Street, was, despite its limitations, agreed to be the best the BBC had. It was designed to cater for a hundred at a time, but it could barely cope: apparently people from up the road at Broadcasting House were using it too. Main meals were cheap, 1s 6d, but because of the war there were some *ersatz* touches to appall a food purist like Orwell. There was only processed milk available; saccharine was on offer to alleviate the shortage of sugar. Winston Smith is amazed when Julia procures him sugar, though curiously he puts it in his coffee.

The Peter Robinson building, 200 Oxford Street, W1.

Turning up the pain in a torture session, or mixing the sound for a broadcast? Aspects of the Ministry of Love, like the Ministry of Truth, are mirrored from the BBC. The ever-lit and windowless recording studios, insulated from the flow of daily life in the basement of the building, were clearly a type for the cells in Miniluv. Room 101 is many metres underground, and within, deceptively innocent, are two tables, 'each covered with green baize'. Tables covered with baize to keep down accidental noise had been ordered for the new studios in Oxford Street.

Dinner-time in the basement canteen at Broadcasting House. On the back wall a poster from Eileen's Ministry of Food urges, 'Grow Vegetables & Salads'.

An exhibition of wartime recipes at the Ministry of Food in Portman Square, W1, where Eileen worked until she and her husband decided to adopt a child.

The George, 55 Great Portland Street, W1 was near the Queen's Hall, until that building was bombed in May 1941, and so was a favoured place of refreshment with members of the BBC and other symphony orchestras. Sir Thomas Beecham christened it 'The Gluepot', because his musicians got stuck here. Rather plusher and somewhat altered from the wartime days it still retains its splendid Victorian mirrors and panels and curtains, besides a worthy range of beers. Julian Maclaren-Ross wrote that 'by walking in there I stood a much better chance of being signed up to write scripts by some radio producer than by having a hundred interviews at executive level.' From here, old BBC men say, seductions begun at lunchtime were transferred to the BBC's Marie Lloyd club, where they could continue through the afternoon – until opening time again.

The Argyll Arms, 18 Argyll Street, W1. It is likely to have been here, just over the road from 200 Oxford Street, that Orwell brought a BBC colleague he seems to have disliked, John Morris. Asked what he would have to drink Morris rather naively said, not a pint of bitter but, 'a glass of beer'. Orwell was scornful. 'You gave yourself away badly,' he revealed afterwards: 'a working-class person would never ask for "a glass of beer".' 'I don't happen to be a working-class person', Morris said. 'No,' Orwell replied, 'but there's no need to boast about it.'

The Senate House, Malet Street, WC1. 'The Ministry of Truth – Minitrue, in Newspeak – was startlingly different from any other object in sight. It was an enormous pyramidal structure of glittering white concrete, soaring up, terrace after terrace, three hundred metres into the air. . . . It was too strong, it could not be stormed. A thousand rocket bombs would not batter it down.'

Known as 'the Big House in Bloomsbury', the University of London Senate House, designed by Charles Holden and completed in 1937, was the model for the exteriors of Orwell's ministries. Its wartime function was suited to such a role, for it housed the Ministry of Information. Graham Greene, who worked there, and met Orwell after the war, wrote recently that it was 'a beacon guiding German planes towards King's Cross and St Pancras stations. Hardly a night passed without the blackout being ignored, and in my area we suffered for it. I wrote a letter to the Spectator with the title "Bloomsbury Lighthouse". . . . Afterwards the lights were dimmed.'

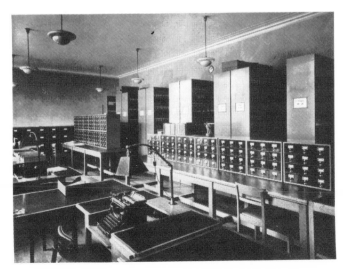

The Central File of the Senate House just after completion – it was to play an important part in the propaganda war. According to Greene the Ministry of Information was much less efficient than the Ministry of Truth: 'To send a minute to anybody else in the great building and to receive a reply took at least twenty-four hours: on an urgent matter an exchange of three minutes might be got through in a week.' As in Miniluv, 'Time outside the Ministry went at quite a different pace.'

Lying or 'black' propaganda was being broadcast from Britain during the war – Orwell's friend Fyvel was engaged in it – but it came from the Foreign Office, not the BBC, which on the whole was merely censored and prejudiced rather than imaginative. Orwell was allowed, as a calculated risk, to cast a fairly individual line to India, and in relation to the 'muck & filth' normally on the air he considered he'd 'kept our little corner of it fairly clean'.

But his attitude was not as simple as that. He seems to have been capable of distributing misinformation himself: 'one rapidly becomes propaganda-minded and develops a cunning one did not previously have. E.g. I am regularly alleging in all my newsletters that the Japanese are plotting to attack Russia. I don't believe this to be so, but . . . I don't think this matters so long as one knows what one is doing, and why.'

His relations with the BBC were difficult and ambivalent. He had both a fascinated fear of the really quite benign Corporation, and a rogue desire to transform it into something truly threatening. A pair of recollections from Mark Benney and Sir William Empson illustrates this:

He enjoyed thinking up horrible conspiracies to which the isolation of a modern communications system could expose him; his own microphone deliberately dead while a voice in a neighbouring booth, using his name, utters shameful and degrading statements, the audience response carefully fabricated to keep the nation's guardian intellects happy though silent;

he found himself having to allow broadcasts to go out to India, from speakers too important to offend, which he thought likely to do more harm than good; well then, the great organization should accept the advice of an Editor, and simply tell the engineers to switch off the power. The man would be thanked and paid as usual, and could be told later if necessary that there had been an unfortunate technical hitch. He seemed genuinely indignant when complaining that the BBC had refused; surely we could not expect to defeat Goebbels, if we were so luxuriously honest as all that.

It seemed likely that hardly anyone was listening anyway, if only because the signal to India was so very weak. When this was suggested to him, Malcolm Muggeridge says, 'the absurdity of the enterprise struck him anew, and he began to chuckle; a dry, rusty, growly sort of chuckle, deep in his throat, very characteristic of him and very endearing.' Eager as he had been for war work two years before, he had now had enough of it. 'At present I'm just an orange that's been trodden on by a very dirty boot'. Working for the BBC had tired and demoralised him, but the imaginative stimulation was to prove to have been invaluable. He left in November 1943, 'after two wasted years', he complained, to become literary editor of an independent socialist paper, *Tribune*. It was a lighter burden and his mood lightened with it.

7

TRIBUNE

The Outer Temple, housing the old *Tribune* offices, is near the joining of Fleet Street and the Strand. This quarter of London was of professional importance to Orwell: he had been there in the early 1930s, interviewing tramps and pavement artists, and again and again, for all manner of reasons, the area proved to be at the hub of his activity.

His first publisher, Victor Gollancz, was here, over the other side of the Strand in Covent Garden. Gollancz was an inspired and innovative man, who discovered Orwell and took on his almost unsaleable novels in the belief that they would eventually be worth his while. He and his author diverged politically over the Spanish Civil War, and he later turned down *Animal Farm* on a matter of political principle. Many people were to find the casting of the Russian leaders as pigs as distasteful as Orwell had found the comparable portrayal of Germans in the First World War.

The Gollancz office is at 14 Henrietta Street, a rambling old building, dominated in those days by Victor's voice and temperament. He was a boisterous employer, continually bawling for attention. A member of his staff, Peggy Duff, remembers that he specialised in shouting. 'He used to lose his temper, temporarily and completely. Once when he was shouting at some luckless boy downstairs, the doorman from the theatre across Maiden Lane came running over, believing a riot was in progress. But his tempers were short-lived. He would scream and shout and then lie down on his easy chair in his room and sleep it off, while everyone else, especially the luckless victim of his wrath, was reduced to jelly. One of his daughters used to imitate V.G. when the bath water was cold. V.G. being cut off on the phone was a similar occasion.'

The premises of Orwell's second publishers, Secker and Warburg, were nearby too, at 22 Essex Street, an elegant Georgian house of dark grey brick. Orwell had been a regular visitor there since 1937, when Fredric Warburg took on *Homage to Catalonia*. In a volume of autobiography he describes the locality:

Essex Street runs south from the Strand, leaving it a few yards east of the church of St Clement Danes, the famous church of the nursery rhyme, 'Oranges and lemons say the bells of St Clement's. Perhaps Orwell's grim use of the rhyme in *1984*. . . can be put down to the frequency with which he was to pass it on the way to our office. The south end of Essex Street, a narrow little road, culminated in the Essex Steps, a steep flight of about eighteen stone stairs leading to the Thames Embankment. Over the steps rose a fine arch; half-way down on the left lay the Steps [*sic*: Stairs] Restaurant, where meals were served by ladies who knew that publishing executives ranked as sweated labour. I often lunched there. No. 22 was the last house but one on the right-hand side going south. As you went in, there was the trade counter. On the first floor were the four rooms which housed what brains and energies the new firm commanded. My own office was long and rather narrow, with a window looking out across the gardens on the Embankment and over the Thames.

He remembered Orwell arriving at this office once in 1940, his clothes baggy and dirty, looking grim, yet cheering up at the thought of privations to come:

I offered him a cigarette. 'I'll smoke my own,' he said, producing a dark twist of tobacco from a pouch, and rolling it deftly in a cigarette paper. I watched with interest. From a capacious pocket he extracted a gigantic piece of apparatus.

'What on earth is that?' I asked him. 'A cigarette lighter,' he said. 'There won't be any wood for matches in a few months' time.' Proudly he showed me the mechanism, which he said he had acquired during his service with the P.O.U.M. militia in the Spanish Civil War. It was awe-inspiring. The chief feature was a rope well over an inch in diameter and three feet long from container to tip. Manipulation produced a dull glow of heat at the end. Not without difficulty he managed to bring the dilapidated business-end of his cigarette into contact with the glow and lit it. The gadget was a triumph of misplaced ingenuity.

'How lucky you are,' I said, 'to have such a wonderful lighter.'

'It is rather neat,' he replied, grinning with pleasure and entirely unconscious of the irony of my compliment. 'I reckon that will last about three-and-a-half years. The war will go on at least as long as that.' A gleam of satisfaction lit up his granite face, as he made this only too modest prophecy. But I never saw him use the thing a second time, the mechanism must have turned out unsatisfactorily.

Now he was working nearby at *Tribune*, a job for which, with his literary, political and editorial experience, he might have been thought well-suited, yet he was rather uncomfortable there. According to Fyvel, 'He sat sadly eyeing a pile of new books for review like a set of enemies.' Peggy Duff joined *Tribune* from Gollancz in early 1949, some little time after Orwell had left. She remembers they worked on the first floor in a suite of five rooms, leading from east to west: the business and circulation office, the general office, the political editors' office, and the literary editor's office. 'Beyond the literary office was the back number store, a dark and dusty purgatory into which we had to delve every time an American academic writing a thesis on George Orwell came in'. George Woodcock would call in at Orwell's small, crowded room and talk to him 'over a desk piled high with books and manuscripts, behind which he looked pent in, with no room for his long legs. The typewriters would clatter in our ears from the neighbouring desks and the V2s would go off in the distance like the rockets falling in *Nineteen eighty-four.*'

'It was interesting,' he wrote, 'but it is not a period that I look back on with pride.' The reviews he commissioned were flat and second-rate, nor did he always commission them: people heard that they could pick up a review copy and a fee simply by calling round at his office. He looked with favour on some fascinatingly bad poetry. He must have been a most idiosyncratic editor, for he hated planning ahead, he said, and had 'a psychical or even physical inability' to answer letters. And because the memory of his early struggle to get into print had not faded, he soft-heartedly filled his pages with material he knew was bad, simply to give an author a break. He explained to Fyvel with serious exaggeration that a small *Tribune* fee might mean the difference to some writers between eating and not eating. He seems to have gone to scarcely credible lengths of benefaction, taking on the part of a Cheeryble: 'I twice caught him', Paul Potts reveals, 'shoving a bank-note into an envelope with the manuscript of a poem, that was too hopelessly bad even for him to be able to print. . . . He looked as guilty when I caught him doing this as he must have when as a small boy he was caught helping himself to the jam.' The long-suffering John Morris found him less generous. He was never paid for the review he did. When he mentioned the fact to Orwell he got a look of faintly mocking surprise. Didn't he know, he was asked, that it was all for The Cause?

Tribune was run in an idealistic but eccentric way. 'In Jon Kimche's recollection,' Fyvel says, 'the weekly editorial meetings were rather like a stage play by Pinter: the participants spoke only in monologues. For instance, Nye Bevan might give a fervent lecture on nationalising the coal industry, his editorial for the week. After this, George would observe how depressing it was getting rid of Hitler only to be left with a world dominated by Stalin, American millionaires and some tinpot dictator like de Gaulle – this would be *his* theme for his weekly "As I Please" column.'

No longer reined in by BBC censorship, and being merely a literary editor on a political paper, Orwell was as free in the composition of his column as its title suggests. It was a popular but provocative feature which he continued to write after he had given up the editorial job. Some doctrinaire readers threatened to cancel their subscriptions because of it, but *Tribune* knew its worth, and paid Orwell five guineas an article, which was more than most people could expect. It was written with winning facility and good humour, so it is a little surprising to learn how seriously Orwell took it. After he had left the paper, Tom Hopkinson was told, he 'would never allow a word of these contributions to be cut by anyone else. He delivered his copy, written to almost exactly the required length, at precisely the agreed time. Next morning he stayed at home so that he could be 'phoned if his copy ran out too long. Once he had made the cuts asked for, nothing must be touched'. On one occasion a tired proof-reader allowed the misprint 'verbiosity' into his piece, which upset him for days.

He would often lunch with friends at the local Bodega wine bar in Bedford Street, just off the Strand. It functioned on two levels. Downstairs was rough and unwashed, full of beer-drinking draymen, but the dark old stairs led to an elite literary civilisation on the first floor. Here publishers, agents, authors and journalists met at lunchtime to eat, gossip, do business, and drink wine by the bottle or glass. On one occasion when Orwell went with George Woodcock, 'the only dish offered was boiled cod with bitter turnip tops. I found the combination of flavours appalling, but Orwell, who extracted a boyish enjoyment out of the hardships of the time, ate his fish and greens with relish. "I'd never have thought they'd have gone so well together!" he remarked reproachfully to me when I sent back my plate almost untasted.'

Here, and at places like it, the subjects of 'As I Please' would sometimes be rehearsed. In his single-toned voice he would talk, to Julian Symons and others, 'almost continuously, but with regard to what was said by his companion, on the immense variety of subjects about which he wrote. His talk, like his journalistic writing, was a mixture of brilliant perception, common sense and wild assertion.' A memoir by Malcolm Muggeridge has preserved just this flavour:

Thus he would come out with the proposition: 'All tobacconists are Fascists!' as though this was something so obvious that no one could possibly question his statement. Momentarily, one was swept along. Yes, there was something in it; those little men in their kiosks handing out fags and tobacco all day long – wouldn't they have followed a Hitler or a Mussolini if one had come along? Then the sheer craziness of it took hold of one, and one began to laugh helplessly, until – such was his persuasiveness – one reflected inside one's laughter; after all, they are rather rum birds, those tobacconists.

In this spirit, Symons says, he might 'identify nationalism with Fascism in the presence of an Irish nationalist, or talk about the corrupting nature of Jewish violence in Palestine in front of an enthusiastic Zionist. It is not easy to convey the offence he gave by his directness, an offence of which he was genuinely unaware, and by which he was always surprised when he discovered it.'

Orwell continued to lunch with Symons and Muggeridge and Powell at the Bodega while he was in London, but in March 1945 he left *Tribune* to take up a job as a war correspondent in Germany for the *Observer*; apparently he badly wanted to have a look at a totalitarian state before it disappeared. Fyvel, who was to take over from him, went round to the Outer Temple to take up the threads. 'I found to my surprise that the drawers of his desk were stuffed with unpublished manuscripts of reviews, literary articles and poems. "What on earth are all these?" I asked. He sighed. "Most of them are unspeakably bad," he said, "but I could not bring myself to send them back."' He knew he had not been a success, but, as he later reflected, 'it was "all experience", as they say, and I have friendly memories of my cramped little office looking out on a back-yard, and the three of us who shared it huddling in the corner as the doodlebugs came zooming over, and the peaceful click-click of the typewriters starting up again as soon as the bomb had crashed.'

Inside Victor Gollancz's offices, 14 Henrietta Street, WC2. The avuncular Gollancz stands over one of his best-selling young authors, 'Cato'. Orwell noted in his diary in July 1940 that 'The book Gollancz has brought out, Guilty Men, *the usual "indictment" of the Munich crowd, is selling like hot cakes.' The angular features of 'Cato' are Michael Foot's.*

The Outer Temple, 222 Strand, WC2. Orwell's friend and successor as literary editor at Tribune, *Tosco Fyvel, standing in the imposing doorway to the paper's first-floor offices.*

St Clement Danes church, Strand, WC2, on fire late in 1940 after a bombing raid. It has since been rebuilt, though it is not in Nineteen eighty-four: *'Winston came across to examine the picture. It was a steel engraving of an oval building with rectangular windows, and a small tower in front. There was a railing running round the building, and at the rear end was what appeared to be a statue. . . "I know that building," said Winston finally. "It's a ruin now. It's in the middle of the street outside the Palace of Justice." "That's right. Outside the Law Courts. It was bombed in – oh, many years ago. It was a church at one time".'*

Essex Steps, WC2. Pictured here before the V1 blast that led to the rebuilding of the area after the war. Fredric Warburg's office is to the left, looking out over the Thames. The sign of the Stairs Restaurant, at which he often lunched, is also visible.

The Law Courts, Strand, WC2. Or, in Nineteen eighty-four, *The Palace of Justice: probably where Jones, Aaronson and Rutherford were tried in the late 1960s.*

(below)
The equestrian statue of Charles I standing in Trafalgar Square on the spot where the regicides were hanged after the Restoration. The king looks down Whitehall to the scene of his own execution. In Nineteen eighty-four *the statue 'was supposed to represent Oliver Cromwell'. In the background is St Martin's-in-the-Fields church: in the novel a museum for propaganda displays, 'scale models of rocket bombs and Floating Fortresses, wax-work tableaux illustrating enemy atrocities, and the like'.*

The Bodega, 2 Bedford Street, WC2. Now redeveloped.

The now disused British Communist Party headquarters, 16 King Street, Covent Garden, WC2. Their windows were so often broken by those not persuaded to their beliefs that they had to be replaced with glass bricks. Orwell came here in late 1936 hoping that the C.P. would facilitate his entry into Spain. The General Secretary, Harry Pollitt, refused, because of Orwell's independent socialist stance; also because he declined to join the International Brigade until he had seen what was happening. He went along instead to the Independent Labour Party, telling Fenner Brockway there that all he wanted to do was 'have a whack' at Franco.

Louis Simmonds in his shop at 16 Fleet Street, EC4. Orwell often used to pop in to sell the books that came his way as a reviewer. The book-seller once asked the author why he had chosen the name he had. Orwell explained that he had wanted an initial letter from the middle of the alphabet. If you came early in the alphabet your books were out of sight on the top shelves of the shop; if you came at the end they were about the customers' feet. 'Orwell' would be at eye level, and sell accordingly.

Early in 1945 he confided that he had had difficulty placing Animal Farm *with a publisher. Simmonds wondered out loud if it really was an appropriate time to bring out an anti-Russian satire. 'Not you as well Simmonds!' Orwell exclaimed, and stormed out of the shop. After reading the book Simmonds changed his mind and became a warm admirer, urging all his customers to buy a copy. He sold a great many.*

The old Freedom Bookshop, 27 Red Lion Street, WC1. The Freedom Bookshop was set up after the war by George Woodcock to provide an anarchist alternative to Collet's communist empire. Orwell was a regular visitor. Queen Elizabeth The Queen Mother's copy of Animal Farm *was bought here, as everywhere else had sold out.*

The Conway Hall, 25 Red Lion Square, WC1. The Conway Hall in the north-eastern corner of Red Lion Square was built in 1929 and is one of London's most charming and eccentric buildings. It is the home of the South Place Ethical Society, a non-doctrinal group offering, among other things, lectures and chamber music. Orwell, a member, addressed a post-war meeting of the Freedom Defence Committee here. Fenner Brockway and George Woodcock were among the other speakers. Symons, who was there too, judges him to have been 'an extremely bad speaker, and I thought at the time how courageous it was on his part to do something that he obviously greatly disliked. He started off the collection with a five-pound note.'

Fleet Street, EC4, Victory over Japan day, 14th August, 1945. 15th August, 1945: 'The news of the Japanese surrender came in yesterday about lunchtime, when I was in Fleet Street. There was quite a bit of jubilation in the streets, and people in upstairs offices instantly began tearing up old papers and throwing them out of the windows. This idea occurred to everyone simultaneously, and for a couple of miles my bus travelled through a rain of paper fragments which glittered in the sunlight as they came down and littered the pavements ankle deep. It annoyed me rather. In England you can't get paper to print books on, but apparently there is plenty of it for this kind of thing.'

The former Observer *offices, Tudor Street, EC4. 'If you ever have to walk from Fleet Street to the Embankment, it is worth going into the office of the* Observer *and having a look at something that is preserved in the waiting-room. It is a framed page from the* Observer *(which is one of our oldest newspapers) for a certain day in June, 1815. In appearance it is very like a modern newspaper, though slightly worse printed, and with only five columns on the page. The largest letters used are not much more than a quarter of an inch high. The first column is given up to "Court and Society", then follow several columns of advertisements, mostly of rooms to let. Halfway down the last column is a headline* SANGUINARY BATTLE IN FLANDERS. COMPLETE DEFEAT OF THE CORSICAN USURPER. *This is the first news of Waterloo!' The page, the only copy the* Observer *had, was stolen from the wall about ten years after Orwell's death. The paper has since moved east to St Andrew's Hill.*

'If you are ever near St Paul's & feel in a gloomy mood, go in & have a look at the statue of the first Protestant bishop of India, which will give you a good laugh.'

8

FATHER AND WIDOWER

In the early summer of 1944, with George still working at *Tribune*, there were domestic changes in the Orwells' lives. Eileen gave up her job at the Ministry of Food so that a baby could be adopted, as her husband so very much desired. Then in late June a doodlebug fell nearby in Mortimer Crescent, and though unhurt they had to move out. For a while they lived in a friend's flat, now demolished, at 106 George Street, W1, near the Ministry Eileen had just left. Finally they moved to Islington and their last London home, at 27b Canonbury Square.

Canonbury Square, and indeed Islington generally, is now expensively restored and sought after. When the Orwells moved in it was bombed about and shabby, and their flat in the south-eastern corner on the top floor was neglected and unwelcoming. Fyvel noted its 'utter cheerlessness' and his wife thought that 'it looked as if every door had a slice at the bottom sawn off so that cold draughts could whistle through the entire flat'. The beauty of its situation, V. S. Pritchett was told, was that one could more easily get out on to the roof to put out fire bombs, if one lived on the top floor. The run-down surroundings were made tolerable for the couple by their child: the pleasure their new son gave them was apparent to all the visitors. But nobody realised just how abnormally weak Eileen had become. Elisaveta Fen found her in the autumn of 1944 'in the back garden trying to wheel the pram with Richard asleep in it into the entrance hall by the stairs. I helped her to get it in, Eileen remarking with a smile: "He's got to be carried upstairs, but the creature's put on so much weight lately that I just can't manage it. . . ." Her remark was one of those warnings one heeds momentarily with a painful contraction of the heart, only to brush aside as unfounded fears. As we drank tea in front of the fire (for which the coal had to be carried up all those flights of steps), and Richard lay on his back on the couch, cooing happily and playing with his toes, his adoptive parents looked more serene, more relaxed and happier than they had done for some time past.'

Orwell was now for the first time, and for only a very brief time, a paterfamilias, and he took a proud joy from entertaining his friends. 'He loved being a host,' Paul Potts thought, 'as only civilised men can, who have been very poor. There was nothing bohemian about him at all.' Potts's description of Orwell's high tea table reveals the dedication with which very ordinary, but traditionally English, foods were served:

Nothing could be more pleasant than the sight of his living room in Canonbury Square at high tea-time. A huge fire, the table crowded with marvellous things . . . various jams, kippers, crumpets and toast. And always the Gentleman's Relish, with its peculiar unique flat jar and the Latin inscription on the label [*Patum Peperium*]. Next to it usually stood the Cooper's Oxford Marmalade pot. He thought in terms of vintage tea and had the same attitude to bubble and squeak as a Frenchman has to Camembert.

In the garden of the Canonbury Tavern, Canonbury Place, N1. 'A street or so from Canonbury Square stood a large working-class tavern, a kind of gin palace, with cut-glass screens and a big garden filled with tables, where the proletarians would sit on a summers' evening in whole families, with the fathers and mothers downing pints of old-and-mild while the children shouted on the swings which the publican had so cannily provided. Orwell liked to go there occasionally, always keeping a weather eye open so that he might avoid the embarrassment of running into one of the little group of Stalinist writers who lived in the district. But he did not appear to know any of the working men who frequented the pub, and he certainly seemed out of place among them, a rather frayed sahib wearing shabby clothes with all the insouciance an old Etonian displays on such occasions.' (George Woodcock, The crystal spirit). The pub seems to be a source of The Moon Under Water, the impossible ideal pub described in an article in 1946. This rusted skeleton is all that remain of the children's swing.

It was becoming difficult to keep a good table, because even as the war was being won, life was getting harder and harder. This was the age, Orwell said, 'of concentration camps and big beautiful bombs', a period of privation at home and horror abroad. Constantine Fitzgibbon has described the London atmosphere towards the end of the war as 'one of exhaustion shot through with violence and hatred. We read about the concentration camps and we wondered which pub would have beer tonight.' After the massive day bombings, and then night bombings, had been called off, London had entered a period of merely routine austerity. The sense of urgency dissolved: in September 1944 a dim-out replaced the black-out, while the Home Guard was stood down in December. But in 1944 too, the flying bombs began to throb over, less materially destructive to London life than the great air-raids, but newly and penetratingly unnerving. The V2 rockets started to drop in September. Cyril Connolly found himself particularly sensitive to them: 'They have made London more dirty, more unsociable, more plague-stricken than ever. The civilians who remain grow more and more hunted and disagreeable, like toads each sweating and palpitating under his particular stone. Social life is non-existent, and those few and petty amenities which are the salt of civilian life – friendship, manners, conversation, mutual esteem – now seem extinct for ever. Never in the whole war has the lot of the civilian been more abject, or his status so low.'

The V1s (or doodlebugs) which preceded them seem to have frightened Eileen as the other bombs had not. She told the novelist Lettice Cooper that, 'George once said in bed at night, "I always know when one is coming right over because I feel your heart beating faster against me".' Orwell himself, who had opened a 1941 pamphlet with the line, 'As I write, highly civilised human beings are flying overhead, trying to kill me', kept calmer about these new and impersonal threats. In December 1944 he told the *Tribune* readers that the V2 'supplies another instance of the contrariness of human nature. People are complaining of the sudden unexpected wallop with which these things go off. "It wouldn't be so bad if you got a bit of a warning" is the usual formula. There is even a tendency to talk nostalgically of the days of the V1. The good old doodlebug did at least give you time to get under the table, etc. etc. Whereas, in fact, when the doodlebugs were actually dropping, the usual subject of complaint was the uncomfortable waiting period before they went off. Some people are never satisfied.'

The waiting period after the engine had cut out was about ten seconds.

Orwell nevertheless realised how much more bearable everyday sufferings were when overshadowed by an external threat. That threat was quickly being eroded by the Allied advance. The Allies crossed the Rhine on 7th March 1945, and Orwell, now an *Observer* correspondent, left for the Continent a week later to see for himself what was happening. Then, at the end of the month, disaster struck and Eileen died, in hospital under anaesthetic for an operation for cancer. Her husband was in Germany.

Orwell's life, often externally bleak, now became inwardly deprived and lonely. Visiting him after his return from Europe, the war over, Fyvel and his wife saw him 'showing his affection for his child amidst surroundings of strange, almost deliberate discomfort, almost background gloom. Looking back I feel one should have sensed that, bereft of Eileen, he was no longer clear about his whole setting in his journalistic London life.'

He had come to London in 1940 with feelings of excitement and duty, both of which had long since flagged. When the promise of the socialist revolution and the threat of German invasion receded he came increasingly to resent London as a place of imprisonment. Nor did he, after August 1945, need London employment, because *Animal Farm* was an instant success. He had been wanting to escape long before Eileen's death. 'I have been tied so tight to this beastly town', he wrote in 1944, 'that for the first time in my life I have not heard a cuckoo this year.' A few years earlier the nightly scenes in the Tube stations had charmed him; now he recorded only his disgust:

about midnight, I came on a little girl of five 'minding' her younger sister aged about two. The tiny child had got hold of a scrubbing brush with which she was scrubbing the filthy stones of the platform, and then sucking the bristles. I took it away from her and told the elder girl not to let her have it. But I had to catch my train, and no doubt the poor little brat would be eating filth in another couple of minutes.

It was not an environment in which he wished his son to grow up.

Though the war was won, material things were short. Anthony Burgess has described the post-war hardship: 'now we had worse privations than during the war, and they seemed to get worse every week. The meat ration was down to a couple of slices of fatty corned beef. One egg a month, and the egg was usually bad. . . . You couldn't get cigarettes. Razor blades had disappeared from the market. . . .

The cheating of the senses with shoddy food, drink and tobacco, the rough clothes, coarse soap, blunt razor blades, the feeling of being unkempt and unclean – it was all there for fictional transference. It was a bad time for the body.' People were ill-provided for in the winter of 1945 – 46, and Orwell suffered from the cold (he had only a ton of coal and no logs), from hack-work, and artistic frustration: 'I am constantly smothered under journalism – at present I am doing 4 articles every week – and I want to write another book which is impossible unless I can get 6 months quiet. I have been in London almost the whole of the war.' For his own sake and for his son's he was determined to escape.

Orwell was not, in a simple way, starry-eyed about the country life; but, without sentiment, he felt deprived away from a garden and from fishing and from the pattern of seasons. For many years he had wanted to live on an island in the Hebrides; in 1944, through David Astor, he travelled up to Jura to view a farmhouse, 'Barnhill', to rent. After the death of Eileen, and living in a flat from which he could not bear to dispose of her things, his incentive to leave was stronger, and from the spring of 1946 to his final hospitalisation he spent as much time as he could in Jura, with his son, his housekeeper, and then later his sister, 'old Av'. Neither the climate there nor the lifestyle were especially injurious to his health in comparison with London. 'Winter is setting in here,' he wrote in October 1947, 'rather dark and gloomy. Already we light the lamps at about half past five. However we've got a lot more coal here than we should have in London, and this house is a lot more weatherproof than my flat, where the water was coming in through the roof in twelve places last winter.' Perhaps more to the point, he was dangerously remote from any kind of medical care.

On his returns to London he was lionised, for he had now become a famous author. Rayner Heppenstall saw him at a party 'surrounded by new friends who called him "George".' Yet it was clear his health was in decline. He spent weeks in bed with bronchitis, only getting up in pyjamas and shaggy dressing-gown, looking 'exceptionally gaunt and pale', Woodcock says, to work at the reviews and articles he was unable to refuse when back in the clutches of the London editors. In Jura, feverishly working at his last novel, he became increasingly fragile and was forced to spend months in hospital near Glasgow. Staying in Scotland, now desperately ill though he would not fully admit it, became an act of perversity. He moved south, to a sanatorium in Gloucestershire in January 1949.

Canonbury Square, Islington, N6. Number twenty-seven is the paler building in the centre of the view. Orwell lived at the top of the house from 1944, first with Eileen, then with a housekeeper, then with his sister Avril. It cost him about £100 a year to rent. Eileen once told a friend that they would be able to afford much better places if they didn't both smoke so much.

Orwell and Richard in the back garden at 27 Canonbury Square.

A V1 about to crash in Drury Lane, 1944. 'What is your first reaction when you hear that droning, zooming noise? Inevitably, it is a hope that the noise won't stop. You want to hear the bomb pass safely overhead and die away into the distance before the engine cuts out. In other words, you are hoping that it will fall on somebody else. So also when you dodge a shell or an ordinary bomb – but in that case you have only about five seconds to take cover and no time to speculate on the bottomless selfishness of the human being.'

The propulsion unit of a V2 at Limehouse, March 1945. 'I am no lover of the V2, especially at this moment when the house still seems to be rocking from a recent explosion, but what depresses me about these things is the way they set people talking about the next war. Every time one goes off I hear gloomy references to the "next time", and the reflection: "I suppose they'll be able to shoot them across the Atlantic by that time".'

Rayner Heppenstall's first floor flat, 38 Rosslyn Hill, NW3. 'Orwell appeared in Rosslyn Hill one Sunday afternoon between Easter and Whitsuntide [1945]. Under his left arm was Richard Horatio. In his right hand he carried a carpet bag, from which, first, a presentation copy of Animal Farm *was extracted. Richard and my son crawled about the floor together and poked at each other's eyes. Out of the carpet bag, from time to time, further came a bottle of orange juice or a change of napkins. . . . After tea, we all trooped down to William Empson's.'*

The Empsons' flat, 160a Haverstock Hill, NW3, famous for its open-house drinking parties, after pub hours.

The former offices of the Freedom Defence Committee, 8 Endsleigh Gardens, WC1. George Woodcock writes that the committee 'led a precarious but active existence from 1944 until 1949. Its leading members were a mixed group of intellectuals, artists and political workers. . . . Bertrand Russell, H. J. Laski, E. M. Forster, Herbert Read, Cyril Connolly, Benjamin Britten, Henry Moore, Osbert Sitwell and Augustus John were among its supporters, and Orwell became vice-chairman.'

It came into being because the National Council for Civil Liberties was strongly influenced by communists and fellow travellers and so chose not to support the causes of those non-communist intellectuals who fell foul of government discrimination.

Collins' Music Hall, 10–11 Islington Green, N1. Orwell once took his housekeeper Susan Watson here after the war. It was opened in 1863 by Sam Collins, stage Irishman and chimney sweep. Chaplin, Lauder, Marie Lloyd, Trinder, Gracie Fields, Wisdom and many others appeared there, before it was burned out in 1958. 'There are music-hall songs which are better than three-quarters of the stuff that gets into the anthologies', Orwell thought:

*'Come where the booze is
   cheaper,
Come where the pots hold
   more,
Come where the boss is a bit of
   a sport,
Come to the pub next door!'*

9

MARRIAGE AND DEATH

In June 1949 *Nineteen eighty-four* was published. Orwell had less than eight months to live. In early September he transferred himself, on the insistence of friends, from the convalescent sanatorium in Gloucestershire to University College Hospital in Gower Street for private treatment of his advanced tuberculosis.

From outside, UCH is an oppressive building of blackened red brick and piping, irregularly steaming and smoking from inner activities. Visitors go in from Gower Street with flowers throughout the afternoon; in the early morning the deceased are driven away from a back entrance. The private patients' wing is just around the corner in Grafton Way. It was Orwell's last hope. Though, as Connolly reports, 'he most bitterly longed to be well', his compulsion to write had taken up energies he might have used for recovery. Only now, when he found not only the physical process of writing exhausting, but the effort of thinking rigorously impossible to sustain, did he try to resign himself to a few years' more life 'at the bath chair level'. 'The one chance of surviving, I imagine, is to keep quiet', he wrote to Warburg. 'Don't think I am making up my mind to peg out', he added; but nevertheless he was taking care to put his affairs in order for his publisher, his adopted son, and his burial. The wistful hope he expressed to friends in these declining months, that a writer could not die when he had books still unwritten, suggests a fantasy of life, not its expectation.

The reason for moving to UCH was the excellence of the treatment it offered, but it meant too that his numerous and anxious friends could visit him more readily. One was Tosco Fyvel:

In the private wing of University College Hospital . . . a square pane of glass was let into the door of each sickroom through which patient and caller could see each other. My first glimpse of Orwell was always through the glass and always with shock at the sight of his thin drawn face looking ominously waxen and still against the white pillows. But then, as I knocked, a sudden slight smile and look of interest would bring his features back to life as he saw that another visitor was calling, and as one entered he would immediately launch into some practical suggestion: 'Hello Tosco, help yourself to a drink. There should be whisky on the sideboard. I've just been reading the usual piece in the *New Statesman* attacking NATO . . . By the way, I've just been listening on the wireless to a talk on Palestine – with all that's going on in the world there's no point in your worrying about Palestine.' His need in this way to plunge straight into conversation, with which I was familiar, was more than ordinary shyness; it had something of the schoolboy about it and to the last, even on his sickbed, Orwell seemed to retain his boyhood traits.

Malcolm Muggeridge made frequent use of the half hour a day that Orwell was allowed visitors and has recorded the visits in a diary:

He looks inconceivably wasted, and has, I should say, the appearance of someone who hasn't very long to live – a queer sort of clarity in his expression and elongation of his features. . . . Sonia Brownell, who is supposed to be going to marry him, came in – large, bouncing girl, quite pleasant, I thought. Somewhat disconcerted because before entering she looked for a long time through the glass at the top of the door.

They were indeed to be married on 13th October, and had been planning it for some time. Orwell had written in August that though he supposed 'everyone will be horrified . . . I really think I should stay alive longer if I were married.'

It was a somewhat bizarre wedding ceremony, with one splash of colour. Orwell had been worried about the dowdy appearance he was presenting to his friends, and had had a word with Anthony Powell about it:

'I really might get some sort of smoking-jacket to wear in bed.' he said. 'A dressing-gown looks rather sordid when lots of people are dropping in. Could you look about, and report to me what there is in that line?' War shortages still persisted where clothes were concerned. Nothing very glamorous in male styles was to be found in the shops. Decision had to be taken ultimately between a jaeger coat with a tying belt, or a crimson jacket in corduroy. We agreed the latter was preferable. . . . Sitting up in bed now, he had an unaccustomed epicurean air. . . .

In this jacket he was married, though first the Archbishop of Canterbury had to grant permission for the ceremony to take place. 'It turned out', Muggeridge says, 'to be quite an elaborate legal procedure getting permission, the intention being, I suppose, to protect dying millionaires from designing nurses.' Deathbed marriages, Orwell informed friends, were not very common. A condition of such a marriage was, apparently to his great delight, that the service be performed by a clergyman. Muggeridge teased him by saying that this he never would have had the face to do voluntarily. After a short service, not too tiring, the party made off for a reception at the Ritz, bringing back a signed menu card for the groom.

So Orwell was married to a famously beautiful and infectiously witty young woman, well-liked though a little feared even then. As a life-prolonging strategy, like the charm of unwritten books, it could not succeed, but without doubt it was a stimulant to his good humour, and sustained his pleasure in 'solid objects and scraps of useless information'. After the wedding, Muggeridge remembers, 'he continued to wear the smoking-jacket in bed. I can see him now in it, sitting up and holding forth about how, when he and Sonia set up house all the kitchen fitments were to be in black rubber.' 'George Orwell really does seem better', his diary records a fortnight afterwards: 'George said that he thought old people should be allowed to commit suicide and that "health and beauty" were essential to the good life. . . . He pointed to an advertisement for men's underwear in the evening paper which showed the god Mercury wearing a new brand of underpants, and said that such blasphemy hurt his feelings much more than mockery of the Christian religion.'

But before long the patient's public cheerfulness was becoming a little ghastly. 'Poor George – he went on about the Home Guard, and the Spanish Civil War, and how he would go to Switzerland soon, and all the while the stench of death was in the air, like autumn in a garden.'

Orwell died when his lung haemorrhaged early in the morning of Saturday 21st January 1950. That day he had been due to leave with Sonia for Switzerland. Instead she went round to the Muggeridges' and 'cried and cried'. The funeral was announced in the *Times* the following Wednesday: 'BLAIR – On Jan. 21, 1950, in hospital, ERIC ARTHUR BLAIR (George Orwell). Funeral service at Christ Church, Albany Street, N.W.1, to-morrow (Thursday), at 11 a.m. Flowers may be sent to Leverton & Sons, Ltd., 212, Eversholt Street, Euston, N.W.1.'

It was a melancholy, chilly affair, Muggeridge says:

the congregation largely Jewish and almost entirely unbelievers; Mr Rose, who conducted the service, excessively parsonical, the church unheated. In the front row the Fred Warburgs. Then a row of shabby looking relatives of George's first wife, whose grief seemed to me practically the only real element in the whole affair. The bearers who carried in the coffin seemed to me remarkably like Molotov's boydguard. Tony [Powell] had chosen the lesson from the last chapter of Ecclesiastes, which was very wonderful, I thought, particularly the verse: 'Then shall the dust return to the earth as it was: and the spirit shall return unto God who gave it.' Also the verse ending: '. . . man goeth to his long home, and the mourners go about the streets.'

Interesting I thought, that George should have so attracted Jews because he was at heart strongly anti-Semitic. Felt a pang as the coffin was removed, particularly because of its length, somehow this circumstance, reflecting George's tallness, was poignant.

Read through various obituary articles on George by Koestler, Pritchett, Julian Symons, etc., and saw in them how the legend of a human being is created, because although they were ostensibly correct and I might have written the same sort of stuff myself, they were yet inherently false – e.g. everyone saying George was not given to self-pity, whereas it was of course his dominant emotion.

Meanwhile, as the obituaries were being read, Orwell was making his last escape from London. The long coffin was buried at Sutton Courtenay; as his will directed 'in a country churchyard'. Anthony Powell wondered if he was wearing the crimson jacket.

The University College Hospital private patients' wing, Grafton Way, WC1.

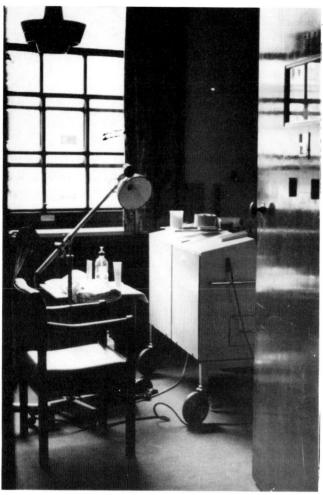

Inside the private patients' wing. Just as in Broadcasting House, one has the illusion here of being in an ocean liner. The engines hum distantly, there is deck upon deck of portholed corridors, panelled in oak. The patients have a much quieter and smoother passage than in the great demotic wards of the main building. They seem mostly to watch television. There was only wireless in Orwell's day, 3s 6d a week extra. Of the original seventy-seven rooms his was number sixty-five (pictured here, top), now used as an office.

When Louis Simmonds came to visit Orwell he would come across Sonia Brownell too. Once he found her and her future husband rather flushed, near the end of a bottle of red wine.

Knowing of her record with Cyril Connolly – among many – Simmonds asked Orwell why he intended marrying her. Orwell explained that it would make things easier with country neighbours.

He was planning a book on Conrad from his hospital bed, and asked his visitor if he would mind getting him a globe, so that he might better envisage Conrad's world. Simmonds laughed him out of it, telling him he'd soon be up and about and able to get one for himself.

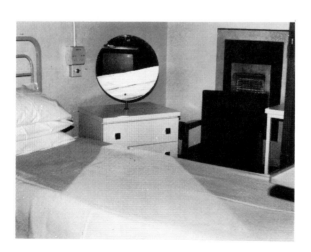

Sonia Orwell (sometimes known as 'the Venus of Euston Road') on her last day at Horizon, *having just married George.*

Leverton & Sons, 210–12 Eversholt Street, NW1, Orwell's undertakers, who, with another branch in Albany Street, had a close business relationship with Rev. Rose of Christ Church. Orwell, who willed that he be buried, disliked the idea of cremation: it was an example of modern degeneracy. In Kentish Town, near the baths he had used, he had seen the cremation advertisement, 'SANITARY. REVERENT. INEXPENSIVE.' applied in an elegant, white enamel arc on the window of an undertaker's. In Keep the aspidistra flying, *which he was writing at the time, he transferred the slogan to Lambeth.*

Christ Church, Albany Street, NW1. This was the first church to be built under Bishop Blomfield's Church Extension Scheme, and was designed by James Pennethorne in 1837. It is a plain brick building with an enormous lofty door. A number of alterations were made thirty years later, including a Rossetti window, illustrating the Sermon on the Mount.

10

NO ENEMY TO PLEASURE —
EATING AND DRINKING WITH ORWELL

George Orwell liked good food, but he liked nasty food too. From child-hood he was attracted by bad, or 'beastly', tastes. Avril says she and her big brother used to knock the seeds out of pine-cones to eat: 'They tasted horribly of turpentine, but we quite liked them.' Jacintha Buddicom tells of penny bags of licorice allsorts, 'tough black leathery things with pink and white sugar stripes which none of us liked. But Eric very occasionally bought them. He said they tasted *so* beastly that they were almost fascinating, and he wanted to make sure they were still as beastly as he had thought. They always were'. The tastes of tramping – skilly and tea-dust tea – and the bitter turnip-tops and watered beer of war must have been curiously satisfying to him as he confirmed his expectation of their unpleasantness.

He was a gourmet of the unpalatable, enjoying it not as a bodily pleasure, but as a kind of penance. Symons observed that 'the more wretched the food served to him the more cheerful he became at doing his bit on the Home Front', that he always chose 'the most synthetic dish, the Victory Pie, as it may have been. After dispatching it he often said with satisfaction, "You won't get anything better than this anywhere."' Circumstances under which the English diet would deteriorate sprang naturally to his mind: rationing extended to bread and beer; England living off herring and potato.

In part his fascination with bad food was a compulsion to face the worst, just as was going to gaol, or down the mine, or thinking about a police state. It was his duty to do these things, and doing them gave him satisfaction and a feeling of achievement. Certainly he was not so obviously perverse as to enjoy the disagreeable and synthetic because he liked the taste. He tried to resist the growing empire of the *ersatz* in 1937, in *The road to Wigan Pier*:

As you can see by looking in any greengrocer's shop, what the majority of English people mean by an apple is a lump of highly-coloured cotton wool from America or Australia; they will devour these things, apparently with pleasure, and let the English apples rot under the trees. It is the shiny, standardised, machine-made look of the American apple that appeals to them; the superior taste of the English apple is something they simply do not notice. Or look at the factory-made, foil-wrapped cheese and 'blended' butter in any grocer's; look at the hideous rows of tins which use up more and more of the space in any food shop, even a dairy; look at a sixpenny Swiss roll or a twopenny ice-cream; look at the filthy chemical by-product that people will pour down their throats under the name of beer.

So although the barely edible intrigued him and caught his imagination, he was a discerning eater. His taste was fastidious and his preparation of food exact. He could be a ritualistic cook, stirring his cocoa only with a wooden spoon, making his tea with measured potency only in a china or earthenware pot, to be shaken, not stirred. Tea-bags appalled him. From his trips north he brought back a liking for oat cakes, potato cakes and black pudding, but not, apparently, for tripe. He liked English cooking, though not out of chauvinism. Living in Paris and working in a hotel kitchen there had left him with international tastes. He did not at all correspond to his idea of typical working-class English people who 'will refuse even to sample a foreign dish', nor with them 'regard such things as garlic and olive oil with disgust'. There is nothing in his life to suggest that his declaration, in *Down and out in Paris and London*, never to enjoy a meal at a smart restaurant was anything more than a resonant way of ending a book.

Much of his eating, and drinking too, was done over a remarkably small area of ground. Many of London's emigré shopkeepers, publicans and restaurateurs had settled themselves into a lively, heterogeneous community in Soho, but some too on the other side of Oxford Street in Fitzrovia. Robert Adam's Fitzroy Square has given its name to this little area. Its main thoroughfare is Charlotte Street, running north and south with, at its southern end, probably the closest concentration of restaurants in London. Here too is the Fitzroy Tavern, once a pub of great character (now unhappily refurnished), and in the popular imagination having as much to do with the naming of the quarter as has the square. Dating from 1897 it had become, by the 1920s and '30s, a meeting-place for artists, dominated by Augustus John, and their hangers-on. Then they thinned out and were replaced by tourists. It was run in Orwell's time by an enormous Russian called Kleinfeld, a man, Fitzgibbon says, 'whose coarse appearance and grossly Mitropa manners concealed a very kind heart: his principal activity, apart from serving drinks and bouncing drunks, was the collection of money to take East End children on seaside outings.' This money was, quite literally, raised: being thrown, pinned, to the ceiling throughout the year and taken down on Twelfth-night, at a big party.

As the clientele of the Fitzroy changed and the pub became only a nominal centre of Fitzrovia, so another pub nearby, the Wheatsheaf, gained the custom of the intelligentsia. Fitzgibbon has it that it was Orwell himself, in 1934, who led the migration from the noisy and crowded house to the Wheatsheaf. It would have been in character: he was always in search of an unspoiled working-class pub in which to make highbrow conversation.

In fact there was a nightly migration from the Wheatsheaf to another pub just across the street, the Marquis of Granby. This was not a first choice for beer and literary talk, since it was run by an ex-policeman and known for its violence; but there was a special reason for going there. The Wheatsheaf and the Fitzroy were in Holborn and licensed only until ten-thirty p.m; the Marquis however, just a few yards further east, was in Marylebone and remained open till eleven. So every night there was a short mass-movement from borough to borough, to join the ex-policeman and his bookmaker friends.

But most of Orwell's eating out and drinking seems, modestly, to have been at lunchtime. In the evenings he was generally in his flat, guarded from visitors by his wife, hammering at his typewriter. Some of his Fitzrovian lunches have become famous. After the publication of *Animal Farm* he took Fredric Warburg to a place in Percy Street:

It was a hot and steamy day. Orwell took off his jacket and hung it over the back of his chair. Almost at once up came the manager to tell him that this conduct could not be allowed in his restaurant. Orwell's reaction was immediate and rather to my surprise fiery. He called the manager a 'bloody fascist'. . . . stood up, put on his jacket, and walked out, leaving me to tag along behind.

In removing his jacket in restaurants he met persistent opposition, which explains the immediate, fiery outburst that surprised Warburg. Before that incident Michael Mayer and Graham Greene had been taken by Orwell to the Elysée in Percy Street. It was chosen because it faced another restaurant, the Akropolis, where the proprietor had insisted Orwell replace his jacket. This man made a habit of standing in his doorway – so Orwell could enter the rival establishment with the satisfaction of being observed. And in the summer of 1946 he explained to Woodcock that he had just begun to patronise a new restaurant because the same thing had happened. There is little doubt that these were all separate incidents: he must have had half the restaurants in the quarter on his blacklist.

Of his conversation at table, Anthony Powell remembers what an excellent companion he was, but that he was easily bored:

If a subject came up in conversation that did not appeal to him, he would make no effort to take it in; falling into a dejected silence, or jerking aside his head like a horse jibbing at a proffered apple. On the other hand, when Orwell's imagination was caught, especially by some idea, he would discuss that exhaustively. He was one of the most enjoyable people to talk with about books, full of parallels and quotations, the last usually far from verbally accurate.

Muggeridge was amused on one occasion by a request his friend made of him:

Once when we were lunching together at a Greek restaurant in Percy Street he asked me if I would mind changing places. I readily agreed, but asked him why. He said that he just couldn't bear to look at Kingsley Martin's corrupt face, which, as Kingsley was lunching at an adjoining table, was unavoidable from where he had been sitting before. . . . I had to admit that I felt no particular distress at having Kingsley in vision.

Martin was the editor of the *New Statesman* who had won Orwell's contempt for his selective discussion of the war in Spain.

Though his eating and drinking were sometimes constrained by the conditions of his life – by hard work, illness, war, and adventures with poverty – he was, as Sir Frederick Ayer has said, 'no enemy to pleasure. He appreciated good food and drink, enjoyed gossip, and when not oppressed by ill-health was very good company.' Ayer writes guardedly, as though he would suggest an ambiguity, and indeed it is not easy to level the notorious bouts of self-punishment with a deep-seated love of life's pleasures. It was a tension Orwell himself recognised and worried away at; he couldn't resolve which side of chicken broth, as he put it, life lies. His admiration for asceticism was confused by an understanding of its inhumanity.

Common friends were aware of the duality but took it less seriously, twinning Orwell with his oldest friend Connolly. Muggeridge records this observation of Powell's: 'George and Connolly, Tony said, were really like two sides of the same face – one lean and ugly and the other fat and ugly; one phoneyly abstemious and the other phoneyly self-indulgent.'

When they first met, Eric was chubby with hamster cheeks, Connolly wide-eyed with Irish charm. They grew up to resemble a kind of double act, and it is pleasant to think of them, Orwell absurdly tall and thin, in proletarian fancy-dress, the sleeves of his jacket seemingly always too short, tucking in to black pudding and mashed potatoes with a 'By Jove, this looks good'; Connolly, sophisticated and self-consciously fat, reluctantly but gamely following suit.

LANDSCAPE WITH FIGURES—IV   OSBERT LANCASTER

A drawing by Sir Osbert Lancaster of intelligent society in the wartime Café Royal, at 68 Regent Street, W1. On the left Stephen Spender is wearing his fireman's uniform; a pimply Cyril Connolly in a check jacket stands towards the centre, while on his right is the pugnacious-looking Kingsley Martin, his mac pocket stuffed with papers from his office in Great Turnstile. Lancaster himself rests his moustache on the balcony.

Orwell began to come to the Café in the 1930s. Lunch could be had for 3s 6d, with dinner two shillings more. Even so, John Betjeman's remembrance of it as scarcely affordable will probably serve for Orwell: 'And there were these marble-topped tables and I was extremely poor and so were most of the people who went there, and the object was to pretend you were going to eat something but really to have a glass of beer and to make it last for about three hours.' Orwell once was roaring drunk here with Richard Rees, a nightmarish episode apparently described in Keep the aspidistra flying.

Later, during the war, the Café was sprinkled with uniforms. In 1941, dressed in 'pretentious regimentals', Anthony Powell was introduced to Orwell who, instead of making the scathing comment Powell expected, tersely enquired, 'Do your trousers strap under the foot?' Powell admitted it. 'Orwell nodded. "That's the really important thing." "Of course." "You agree?" "Naturally." "I used to wear ones that strapped under the boot myself," he said, not without nostalgia.'

The Newman Arms, Newman Passage, Rathbone Street, W1. Small and low-ceilinged, the Newman Arms was formerly known as the Beer House as it had no licence to sell spirits. Houses of this type were exclusively working-class and Orwell was familiar with them. Gordon and Ravelston visit one, to the latter's dismay; and at another Winston vainly tries to discover the truth about life before the revolution.

Looking over at Bertorelli Brothers' restaurant from the Fitzroy Tavern, Charlotte Street, W1. Bertorellis' was founded in 1912 by four brothers, and is now managed by a son of a co-founder, Dante Bertorelli. In 1935 Heppenstall and Dylan Thomas were invited to dine here with Richard Rees. Rees's other guest, Heppenstall says, was 'a tall, big-headed man, with pale-blue, defensively humorous eyes, a little moustache and a painfully snickering laugh'.

The Wheatsheaf, Rathbone Place, W1. The Wheatsheaf has retained its original wood and glass, but lost the decorative tartans that accompanied the Younger's Scotch Ale. The Ale is well remembered by many of Orwell's generation. He himself had fixed ideas about what his friends should drink in a pub. Lettice Cooper recalls that 'whenever I asked for lager or light ale I always got the darkest kind of beer if George was ordering. I protested and Eileen said "It's no use, once you are established as a friend of his you become the kind of person who wouldn't drink lager or light ale and nothing will shake him".'

The Marquis of Granby, Rathbone Street, W1.

The Elysée, 13 Percy Street, W1. 'A group of us', Koestler says, 'used to meet twice or three times a week in the Elysée. The group consisted of David Martin who had been in the Canadian Air Force, Julian Symons, Malcolm Muggeridge, Tosco Fyvel and Orwell. It was in this restaurant that George said about a moussaka (which was a bit of awful Greek cooking, as opposed to the good sort of Greek cooking) that "in all London there wasn't anywhere else that you could get food like that". George had no taste in food.'

18 Percy Street, W1, where Sonia Brownell had her flat and Orwell would visit her. Perhaps these meetings were a model for Winston's and Julia's in Mr Charrington's room.

Lyons' Corner House, 7–10 Strand, WC2. 'We five-to-ten-pound-a-weekers aren't well served in the way of eating-places in London. If your idea of the amount to spend on a meal is one and threepence, it's either Lyons, the Express Dairy or the A.B.C.' (Coming up for air).

There were four Lyons' Corner Houses in London: in the Strand, Coventry Street, Tottenham Court Road, and at Marble Arch. In the 1940s they were serving fifty million meals per year. Their bakeries rolled out ten miles of swiss roll each day, and manufactured many millions of 'Frood' meals. 'Frood' meant 'frozen cooked' food.

The ABC (Aerated Bread Corporation) was the pioneer of teashops, with its first near London Bridge in 1880. By Orwell's time there were 162 branches. Similarly, the Express Dairy Company began opening restaurants in the 1890s. One of these, in Museum Street near the British Museum, was popular with the bookish, and is most probably where Orwell went with Richard Rees on the first occasion they met.

The milk bar was part of Orwell's complaint with the times: 'Everything slick and shiny and streamlined: mirrors, enamel and chromium plate whichever direction you look in. Everything spent on the decorations and nothing on the food. No real food at all. Just lists of stuff with American names, sort of phantom stuff that you can't taste and can hardly believe in the existence of. Everything comes out of a carton or a tin, or it's hauled out of a refrigerator or squirted out of a tap or squeezed out of a tube.' Milk bars became very common between the wars. There were two rival chains: those of Hugh D. McIntosh, who opened his first premises, the Black and White, in Fleet Street in 1935; and Charles Forte, who offered food as well as milk shakes and ice-creams.

The Dog and Duck, Bateman Street, W1. When he heard that the American Book of the Month Club had selected Animal Farm *Orwell rang up his impecunious friend Woodcock to ask him out to a celebratory meal. They had a lavish lunch in Percy Street, with aperitifs, wine and brandy. The bill was an extremely large one – about six guineas – and Woodcock felt obliged to make a complementary gesture. He took Orwell to the Dog and Duck (the name of which commemorates Soho's old hunting associations), tiny and crowded as it is today, which had 'mysteriously acquired a cache of real absinthe'. Against closing time and the press of beer drinkers it was served by having water slowly dripped into it through a cube of sugar. Woodcock sensed Orwell's growing discomfiture: ordering such an ostentatious drink did nothing for his idea of himself as an honorary proletarian. As soon as their glasses were filled they drank them off quickly and hurried out.*

The York Minster or 'French pub', Dean Street, W1. The French pub, favoured by the literati, was made famous by the publican Victor Berlemont who, Fitzgibbon writes, 'with huge and curving moustachios that recalled Napoleon's Old Guard, presided behind an exotic glass contraption that could drip water into four Pernods simultaneously.' He was succeeded, around 1940, by his son Gaston.

The Hungarian Czarda, 77 Dean Street, W1. 'Once you're in here you'll forget there's a war on, business as usual is the proprietor's motto. All the best-loved Hungarian and Viennese dishes, including Chicken Paprika with the traditional pink sauce. Also authentic Goulash. Don't miss the chance to try the heavenly Tokays and other national wines and spirits.' Orwell lunched frequently at the Czarda, which opened in 1937, once with an Oxford friend of Michael Mayer, Graham Greene. 'They conversed so eagerly that when the restaurant closed we continued in a pub across the road called the Crown and Two Chairmen.' (left) Arthur Koestler remembered 'arranging to meet George for dinner in the Hungarian Czarda restaurant in Soho and George came wearing a shirt with a collar which was not just frayed but so torn that people gasped at seeing someone enter the restaurant dressed like that'.

INDEX OF PLACES